A Traveller's Guide to the
BATTLEFIELDS OF BRITAIN

A Traveller's Guide to the
BATTLEFIELDS OF BRITAIN

Neil Fairbairn & Michael Cyprien

HTI

Historical Times INC.
Harrisburg

CONTENTS

First Published in 1983 by Evans Brothers Limited

Published in the United States and Canada
by Historical Times Incorporated
by special arrangement with Bell & Hyman Publishers
Denmark House, 37/39 Queen Street, London SE1 2QB

Text by Neil Fairbairn
Photography and Art Direction by Michael Cyprien
Designed by John Pallot

Typeset in Souvenir by SX Composing Limited, Rayleigh, Essex
Printed in the United States of America
First American Edition

ISBN 0 237 45656 7

INTRODUCTION

The places where society suffered its greatest upheavals are often those that are most easily overlooked. There is nothing inherently dramatic in the lie of the land where thousands of men once assembled to make war. The dull farmland bordering the A6094 south of Musselburgh in Scotland, for instance, is an unpretentious resting place for the Scots who fell on Black Saturday in 1547. Naseby in Northamptonshire seems far too peaceful a spot for the grim battle that effectively ended the Civil War in England. Motorists on the B1217 in North Yorkshire may never have noticed the battered stone column that stands at the side of the road on a low hill near Towton. It bears nothing to record that it marks the site of the bloodiest battle ever fought in Britain where, on a snowy March day in 1461, more than 20,000 men and boys lost their lives.

A Traveller's Guide to the Battlefields of Britain aims to draw attention to the unassertive records of history that surround us in these fields and hillsides. As well as illustrating the text, the photographs included are central to the idea that landscape is a bridge between the past and the present, a memorial more durable than any obelisk or statue.

For the less historically minded, the guide is a reminder that the battlefields of Britain are good places just to stretch your legs or exercise your family. And because armies so often gathered on heights before battle, there is often a walk with a view. Where possible, suggestions have been included for visiting the battlefields on foot in the text accompanying the maps. The rolling farmland near Alresford in Hampshire and Offham Hill above Lewes can be enjoyed quite apart from the fact that important battles were fought there.

Two guiding principles in the selection of these battlefields have been the historical importance of the battle, and the physical nature of the field today. Every effort has been made to include a number of famous fields mistreated by time as, for example, Tewkesbury and Culloden. Some important fields have changed too much to make a visit there rewarding and on this basis, sadly, Evesham, St. Albans and Worcester have been discarded.

Other fields involve difficulties of access. In many cases the landowners (often very knowledgeable about local history) are delighted to allow discreet and interested tourists on to their property, but would not appreciate the publication of a walkers' guide to their gardens, pastures and chicken runs. In Scotland, which has no law of trespass, the owners of the land where the Battle of Killiecrankie was fought have found four words – "Beware of the Bull" – cast a peculiar spell over potential visitors, whether or not they can see a bull. In England and Wales, readers are directed to walk on public rights of way.

Battlefields which are more the product of myth and scholarly one-upmanship than of certainty of location have been omitted. This applies to many of the battles fought before the Norman invasion, when writers of contemporary history were often totally unfamiliar with the places they described.

A Traveller's Guide to the Battlefields of Britain relies where it can upon original sources, while striving at the same time both to avoid controversy and to entertain. Any major dispute regarding location or the nature of the action is acknowledged in the notes on page 156.

Battles are beguiling things. There is a continual temptation to emphasize the heroic, the noble, and even the humane, when one is in fact writing about barbarity and suffering. It is hoped that from these accounts will emerge not just the undeniable romance but, even more, the horror or a sense of what Wilfred Owen called "the pity of war."

Battle Plans
Diagrams that accompany each battle give only a simplified view of how the armies were deployed. They represent the field prior to battle and are superimposed on a modern plan of the area.

LOCATION OF THE FIELDS

The following list of fields includes a number not described in the book (indicated here in light typeface). This is either because they are not immediately rewarding to visit or because access is in some way restricted. It is best to approach such battlefields well-armed with knowledge or initiative.

1 Ashdown – 871 p12.
2 Ethandun – 878 p16.
3 Maldon – 991 p18.
4 Ashingdon – 1016 p22.
5 Stamford Bridge – 25 September 1066. The Norse Invasion. King Harold defeats the Vikings less than three weeks before his own defeat at Hastings. Humberside. SE 7255. O.S. 105.
6 Hastings – 1066 p24.
7 The Standard – 1138 p28.
8 Lewes – 1264 p30.
9 Evesham – 4 August 1265. The Barons' War. Simon de Montfort loses his life against the forces of King Henry III. Hereford and Worcester. SP 0345. O.S. 150.
10 Stirling Bridge – 11 September 1297. The Wars of Scottish Independence. Defeat of a huge English army by William Wallace. Central Region. NS 7895. O.S. 57.
11 Kildrummy Castle – 1306 p34.
12 Brander – 1309 p36.
13 Bannockburn – 24 June 1314. The Wars of Scottish Independence. Major victory for Robert Bruce over Edward II. Central Region. NS 8191. O.S. 57.
14 Boroughbridge – 16 March 1322. The Rebellion of the Marches. The rebel earls Hereford and Lancaster are defeated by the army of Edward II. North Yorkshire. SE 3967. O.S. 99.
15 Halidon Hill – 1333 p38.
16 Neville's Cross – 17 October 1346. The Anglo-Scottish Wars. The Scots under King David II are crushed by Henry de Percy and Ralph de Neville. Durham. NZ 2642. O.S. 88.
17 Otterburn – 1388 p42.
18 Pilleth – 1402 p44.
19 Homildon Hill – 1402 p46.
20 Shrewsbury – 1403 p50.
21 Harlaw – 24 July 1411. The Scottish Civil Wars. Clash between two huge armies. Both sides claim victory, but the rebel Highlanders under Donald, Lord of the Isles, are forced to withdraw. Grampian Region. NJ 7524. O.S. 38.
22 St. Albans I – 22 May 1455. The Wars of the Roses. Defeat of Henry VI's army by the Yorkists under the Earl of Warwick. Hertfordshire. TL 1407. O.S. 166.
23 Blore Heath – 1459 p52.
24 Northampton – 10 July 1460. The Wars of the Roses. Defeat and capture of Henry VI by the Yorkists. Northamptonshire. SP 7559. O.S. 152.
25 Wakefield – 1460 p54.
26 Mortimer's Cross – 1461 p56.
27 St. Albans II – 17 February 1461. The Wars of the Roses. Defeat of the Earl of Warwick by the Lancastrian army of Queen Margaret. Hertfordshire. TL 1610. O.S. 166.
28 Towton – 1461 p60.
29 Hedgely Moor – 25 April 1464. The Wars of the Roses. An inconclusive skirmish in which Sir Ralph Percy, a Lancastrian leader, dies. Northumberland. NU 0419. O.S. 81.
30 Hexham – 15 May 1464. The Wars of the Roses. Rout of Lancastrian army and death of the Duke of Somerset. Northumberland. NY 9561. O.S. 87.
31 Edgcote – 1469 p64.
32 Barnet – 14 April 1471. The Wars of the Roses. Edward IV's Yorkist army defeats and kills the Earl of Warwick. Hertfordshire. TQ 2497. O.S. 176.
33 Tewkesbury – 1471 p66.
34 Bosworth – 1485 p70.
35 Stoke – 1487 p74.
36 Flodden – 1513 p78.
37 Ancrum Moor – 1545 p82.
38 Pinkie – 1547 p86.
39 Wrotham Hill – 1554 p90.
40 Corrichie – 28 October 1562. Huntly's Rebellion. Queen Mary's forces defeat the Earl of Huntley's short-lived rebellion. Grampian Region. NJ 6902. O.S. 38.
41 Langside – 13 May 1568. Scottish Rising Against Mary. Defeat of Queen Mary's army. She retreats to England. Strathclyde Region. NS 5861. O.S. 64.
42 Newburn – 28 August 1640. Anglo-Scottish Wars. A huge Scottish army beat the English back from Newburn Ford and occupy Newcastle. Northumberland. NZ 1665. O.S. 88.
43 Edgehill – 23 October 1642. The Civil War. The first battle of the Civil War tips marginally in favour of King Charles I's Royalists. Warwickshire. SP 3549. O.S. 151.
44 Bradock Down – 19 January 1643. The Civil War. Defeat of Parliamentarian army by Royalists under Sir Ralph Hopton. Cornwall. SX 1561. O.S. 201.
45 Stratton – 1643 p92.
46 Chalgrove Field – 1643 p94.
47 Adwalton Moor – 30 June 1643. The Civil War. Defeat of a Parliamentarian army by the Earl of Newcastle. West Yorkshire. SE 2228. O.S. 104.
48 Lansdown Hill – 1643 p96.
49 Roundway Down – 1643 p99.
50 Newbury I – 1643 p102.
51 Winceby – 11 October 1643. The Civil War. Victory for the Parliamentarian army of Oliver Cromwell and Sir Thomas Fairfax. Lincolnshire. TF 3168. O.S. 122.
52 Newark – 21 March 1644. The Civil War. Prince Rupert's Royalists defeat the Parliamentarians and take the city. Nottinghamshire. SK 8055. O.S. 121.
53 Cheriton – 1644 p106.
54 Cropredy Bridge – 1644 p110.
55 Marston Moor – 1644 p112.
56 Lostwithiel – 1644 p115.
57 Newbury II – 1644 p118.
58 Inverlochy – 2 February 1645. The Civil War. Victory for Montrose over Covenanters under Duncan Campbell. Highland Region. NN 1275. O.S. 41.
59 Auldearn – 1645 p122.
60 Naseby – 1645 p126.
61 Alford – 1645 p130.
62 Langport – 1645 p132.
63 Kilsyth – 15 August 1645. The Civil War. Defeat of Covenanters by Montrose's Royalists. Strathclyde Region. NS 7478. O.S. 64.
64 Philiphaugh – 13 September 1645. The Civil War. Defeat of Montrose's Royalists by David Leslie. Borders Region. NT 4528. O.S. 73.
65 Rowton Heath – 24 September 1645. The Civil War. Royalist defeat outside Chester. Cheshire. SJ 4464. O.S. 117.
66 Preston — 17-19 August 1648. The Civil War. Complete defeat of an outnumbered Royalist army. Lancashire. SD 5532. O.S. 102.
67 Dunbar – 3 September 1650. Cromwell's Scottish Campaign. Defeat of Scottish Royalists. Lothian Region. NT 6976. O.S. 67.
68 Worcester – 3 September 1651. The Civil War. Defeat of Royalist army under the future Charles II. Last major battle of the Civil War. Hereford and Worcester. SO 8452. O.S. 150.
69 Bothwell Bridge – 22 June 1679. Covenanters' Rising. Defeat of the Covenanters by the Duke of Monmouth. Strathclyde Region. NS 7157. O.S. 64.
70 Sedgemoor – 1685 p134.
71 Killiecrankie – 27 July 1689. The Jacobite Rising. Defeat of Royalists loyal to William of Orange by Highland Jacobites. Tayside Region. NN 9063. O.S. 43.
72 Glen Coe – 1692 p138.
73 Sheriffmuir – 1715 p140.
74 Glen Shiel – 1719 p142.
75 Prestonpans – 21 September 1745. The Second Jacobite Rebellion. Defeat of Government forces by Jacobites. Lothian Region. NT 4074. O.S. 66.
76 Clifton Moor – 18 December 1745. The Second Jacobite Rebellion. The retreating Scots hold off an English army. Westmorland. NY 5326. O.S. 90.
77 Falkirk – 1746 p146.
78 Culloden – 1746 p148.
79 Ruthven Barracks – 1746 p152.

Main road
Motorway

0   25   50   75   100 ml

Inverness
59
78
74   11 61
79
72
12
Oban
73
77   38
Glasgow Edinburgh
15
36 19
37
17
Newcastle
Carlisle
7
55 York
28
Leeds
25
Liverpool Manchester
Sheffield
35
23
20
Shrewsbury Leicester Norwich
34
Birmingham 60
18 Ipswich
26 54
31
33
Oxford
46
1 LONDON
3
4
48 Cardiff Bristol 49 57 39
Bath 50
2
53
70 8 6
62 Southampton
45 Exeter Brighton
Plymouth
56

11

The Battle of Ashdown

No one knows precisely where King Ethelred and his brother Alfred, leaders of the Wessex Saxons, routed the Danes in 871. The battle at Aescesdun, or Ashdown, could have been fought at a number of points west of Reading. There are no earthworks, fortresses, memorials or cemeteries to oblige the military historian. Most educated guesses, however, have fixed on the high land of the Berkshire Downs as a likely region for the conflict. Downland makes excellent strategic sense, and for the interested layman it has the added advantage of providing fewer hindrances to the imagination than any other type of terrain. Even to a visitor completely ignorant of history, the chalk tracks, the black clumps of trees and the broad, quiet views in all directions have a timeless serenity. It is

easy to imagine that the Ridge Way, the backbone of these downs, has been a thoroughfare since long before Alfred's day. Saxon armies still seem as appropriate to these fields as hikers or combine harvesters.

If the exact place is uncertain, the events of the battle itself have been convincingly recorded. At the end of the year 870 the relentless Danes, led by Kings Bagsac and Halfden, advanced far into Saxon Wessex, taking the town of Reading, or Raedig as it was then. King Ethelred and his brother Alfred (who, as king, became known as "the Great") quickly organized a counter-attack, but after success in an initial skirmish they were defeated and forced to retreat west into their own territory. The Danes followed them, anticipating total victory, but on the

eighth of January they confronted a revitalized Saxon army at Ashdown. They divided their forces into two halves; the Saxons did the same. Then the Danes began their attack. Amazingly, King Ethelred did not respond. He had ordered a special mass that morning and *"ever would he say,"* wrote a contemporary, *"that never while he lived would he leave his Mass before the Priest had ended it."* This left Alfred, who was only eighteen, in a terrible dilemma. Should he wait for his devout brother or meet the enemy himself? He chose the latter course and startled the Danes with an abrupt and determined charge. *"This way and that swayed the battle for a while,"* wrote Bishop Asser, but when Ethelred arrived, refreshed by prayer, the Danes broke and fled back to Reading, pur-

Lowbury Hill, where the Battle of Ashdown was fought, is on open downland in Berkshire, fifteen miles north-west of Reading. Access to the battlefield is from the B4009 at Aldworth or from the A417, half a mile north of Streatley.

War	The Danish Invasions.
Date	8 January 871.
Principal commanders	Anglo-Saxons: King Ethelred and his brother Alfred. Danes: Kings Bagsac and Halfden.
Size of armies	Unknown.
Duration	Unknown.
Outcome	Defeat of the Danes, resulting in a period of relative peace for the Saxons of Wessex.
County	Berkshire.
Ord. Survey	1:50,000 map no. 174.
Nat. grid ref.	SU 5481.

sued until darkness by the Saxons. King Bagsac lay dead alongside five of the Danish earls.

Of the several sites that have been considered for the Battle of Ashdown, the area just west of Streatley is a most attractive candidate. The summit of Lowbury Hill, the highest point for several miles in any direction, would have served as an ideal observation point for the Saxon army. Looking east from the summit today one could still detect any approach along the Ridge Way from the thick cover of Ham and Unhill Woods. The fields to the south and the east have both been proposed as scenes of battle. Today they are all under cultivation, in January (the month when the battle was fought) presenting a forbidding expanse of tilled earth with the texture of per-

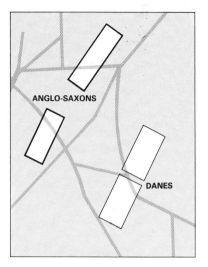

ANGLO-SAXONS

DANES

petually wet cement. In summer the scene is softened by barley and wheat and by the wild-flowers that still thrive along the edges of the fields: forget-me-nots, poppies, wild roses, elder and hawthorn. These hawthorns, which fringe the fields and tracks, may well be descendants of a solitary thorn tree which, according to Bishop Asser, was a centre of much of the fighting. The tree was remembered two centuries later, for the Domesday Book identifies the place where the Ridge Way crosses the road from Starveall Farm as Nachededorn, meaning Naked Thorn. For all the abundance and beauty of the fields today, here at this cross-road it is still possible to evoke the grim vision of a naked thorn and crimson soil when *"dead bodies were strewn all over the plain of Ashdown"*.

A view from the east side of Lowbury Hill (above) looking towards Unhill Bottom. Unhill Wood crowns the far ridge; beyond it is the Ridge Way, an ancient downland track.

Hawthorns prosper near Lowbury Hill, as they did in 871 when the Danes met the Saxons at Ashdown.

To reach the battlefield of Ashdown take the A329 north from Reading, turning left on the B4009 at Streatley. At the village of Aldworth, two and a half miles along this road, turn right and continue on a lane marked "To the Downs". This is paved for about two miles, until just after Starveall Farm. For another half mile the track is generally passable, but where it crosses the Ridge Way it is advisable to continue your exploration on foot. This cross-roads is the point called Nachededorn, the centre of the battlefield, where it is believed a solitary thorn once grew. Lowbury Hill, an observation point for the Saxons, rises gently to the right. A walk of half a mile along the track that lies straight ahead takes you very near the summit. From here you may be tempted to continue straight for a long walk to Langdon Hill, but if you bear left you will reach the trig point that marks the top of Lowbury Hill (610 ft.). There are splendid views to the north and west, but it is the east that the Anglo-Saxons regarded most apprehensively. The confident Danes probably chose to advance along the point of highest land, today partly covered by Ham and Unhill Woods.

Continue walking downhill towards the Ridge Way again. At the cross-roads turn left and return towards Nachededorn. These are the fields which some historians believe were the scene of Alfred's successful attack.

There are a myriad of rights of way and tracks, which provide long walks and longer views on these downs. The Ridge Way itself, one of the most accessible long-distance footpaths in Britain, ends in Wiltshire, forty miles to the west. O.S. map no. 174 (1:50,000) is an indispensable companion for more ambitious rambles.

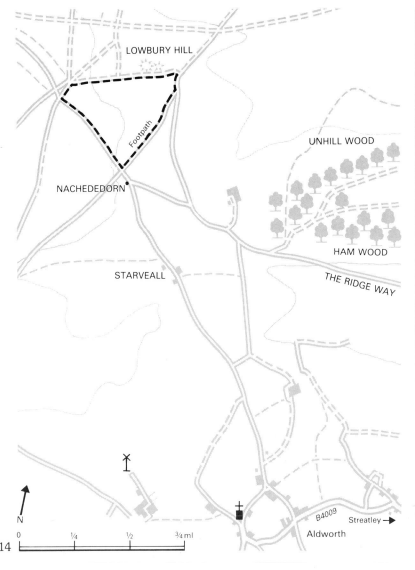

The gentle slopes of Lowbury Hill, upon which
the army of Ethelred awaited the advancing Danes.
(left and below)

15

The Battle of Ethandun

Ethandun is generally believed to be an early form of the word Edington. A village of that name, which suits what little is known of the battle, is in Wiltshire on the B3098, three and a half miles east of Westbury.

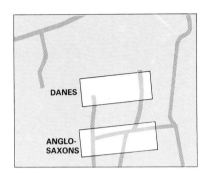

War	The Danish Invasions.
Date	Early summer 878.
Principal commanders	Anglo-Saxons: King Alfred ("the Great"). Danes: King Guthrum.
Size of armies	Unknown.
Duration	Unknown.
Outcome	Defeat of Danes and conversion of King Guthrum to Christianity.
County	Wiltshire.
Ord. Survey	1:50,000 map no. 184.
Nat. grid ref.	ST 9252.

The Battle of Ethandun was a critical event in British history. It shattered the Danish advance and established King Alfred as undisputed ruler of the west of England. Yet little is known about how or even where this crucial battle was fought. *The Anglo-Saxon Chronicle,* a collection of manuscripts that gives a terse political history of England from the fifth to the twelfth centuries, is the principal source of information. Alfred the Great, it tells us, summoned an army from Somerset, Wiltshire and Hampshire, proceeded to Edington, *"and there fought against the whole army and put it to flight".*

And that is just about all we know. Fortunately, the *Chronicle* is not so reticent about the situation immediately before the battle. Alfred, who had been conducting a guerilla war from the swamps of Somerset, was advancing from the south; the Danes had wintered at their camp in Chippenham. There is still a village of Edington, just under the northern slopes of Salisbury Plain, at a point midway between the Danes and the Saxons. Sparse as these clues are, it is safe enough to assume that Edington in Wiltshire is where the two armies met in the early summer of 878.

The downland above Edington allows the imagination a splendid opportunity to create battlefields. Two hills rise up immediately south of the town. Tinhead Hill to the east is the taller. The cornfields of its slopes converge on a solitary tuft of trees at the summit. Edington Hill stands directly above its namesake town, its steep face ribbed with sheep tracks. It would have presented a formidable barrier to any army approaching from the direction of Chippenham. But it is unlikely that the Danes allowed themselves to be forced into such an inferior position. Learning from their scouts that Alfred had emerged from his island retreat of Athelney in Somerset and was mustering an army directly to the south, they doubtless advanced towards Edington in order to gain equality on the high land of Salisbury Plain. The battle may well have taken place on one of the graceful fields behind the summits of these hills, though some historians feel that Bratton Castle, a magnificent hill fort two miles to the west, makes a more appropriate setting. The view to the north here is marvellous and includes the distant Roundway Down where, 800 years later, Parliamentary and Royalist cavalry fought a savage battle. On the slopes of Bratton Castle is the white horse of Westbury. The original animal was long reputed to have been made by Alfred to commemorate his victory. The present horse is a timid looking creature, seen to best advantage from the road below. Up close, he has an ungroomed appearance, the grass sprouting through his vast concrete flanks.

Alfred pursued his opponents to Chippenham, where he besieged them *"and seized all things which he found outside the fort,"* wrote his friend Bishop Asser, *"men and horses and cattle, and slew the men at once."* King Guthrum of the Danes was clearly impressed by this display of severity. At a baptismal ceremony following his surrender, he formally exchanged a pantheon of Norse gods for the fierce Christ of the Saxons.

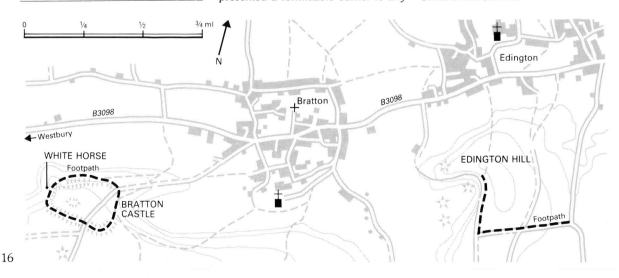

If King Alfred were advancing north through Salisbury Plain today, he would stand a good chance of being shot to pieces in the Ministry of Defence firing ranges which cover so much of the area. Having reached the northern edge of downland, however, he could wage war in peace. The public still have access to the land immediately south of Bratton and Edington.

To reach Bratton Castle and the white horse, drive east along the B3098 from Westbury. At Bratton, in just over two miles, turn right up a steep lane sign-posted to the horse. The castle is a massive earthwork with a magnificent view from its northern walls. The white horse, with its mangy sides and cartoon eyelashes, looks a huge, pathetic beast from this angle. If Alfred held Bratton Castle, it is not surprising that he won the battle. More likely the Danes occupied this stronghold, blocking Alfred's advance from the south.

To reach Edington Hill, another possible site for the battle, continue along the B3098 for a mile and a half, turning right up a lane in the village of Edington. In a thousand yards follow a track to the right (marked Westbury). In 600 yards a gate to the right leads to the uneven summit of Edington Hill. Tinhead Hill is to the east, a broad shoulder of downland with a clump of trees on its summit. Below you to the north is the plain over which Alfred pursued the Danes after his victory.

Despite the amount of land fenced off by the MOD, this edge of Salisbury Plain is rich in walks. A network of rights of way fringe the downland and connect with the western end of the Ridge Way, a path which extends across five counties to Hertfordshire.

O.S. map number 184 reveals a wealth of potential excursions.

At close range, the gigantic white horse of Westbury appears to need a grooming. He stands on a hill fort called Bratton Castle, one possible location for the Battle of Ethandun.

The Battle of Maldon

On the eighteenth of May 1769 a huge, headless skeleton was discovered under a tomb in Ely Cathedral. Measurements indicated that the owner of these bones had once stood six feet nine inches tall. A lump of wax replaced his head, and a contemporary witness observed that *"the collar-bone had been neatly cut through, as by a battle-axe or two-handed sword."* It was widely believed that these were the shattered remains of Britnoth, celebrated leader of the Anglo-Saxons in the east of England and tragic hero of the Battle of Maldon.

Britnoth was an old man, well into his sixties, when the Danes appeared off the coast of Essex in the summer of 991. But he was an inspirational general and a renowned patriot to whom the frightened citizens naturally turned when confronted with these savage raids. *"He was eloquent in speech, of robust strength, and of commanding stature,"* wrote an admiring monk, *"and above all he honoured the holy church and its ministers."* It is

Maldon is in Essex on the estuary of the River Blackwater, ten miles east of Chelmsford.

War	The Danish Invasions.
Date	11 August 991.
Principal commanders	Anglo-Saxons: Britnoth. Danes: Justin and Guthmund.
Size of armies	Unknown.
Duration	All day.
Outcome	Defeat of the Anglo-Saxons. Death of Britnoth.
County	Essex.
Ord. Survey	1:50,000 map no. 168.
Nat. grid ref.	TL 8605.

At low tide the Blackwater Estuary recedes, stranding Northey Island in a muddy plain. The only firm footing, now as in 991, is a causeway, submerged at high water.

no wonder that *"all the chieftains of the neighbouring provinces . . . had pledged themselves to serve beneath his victorious banner."*

It is extremely difficult for an army on land to compete with the swift and unpredictable manoeuvres of an enemy at sea. Britnoth and his men finally caught up with their opponents near Maldon in Essex, but it is likely that the Danes had by then decided to stand and fight. They had successfully ravaged the east coast and sacked the city of Ipswich. Confident that they could win even more spoils in a pitched battle, they disembarked on Northey Island in the River Blackwater and waited for Britnoth.

Northey Island is a marshy triangle consisting largely of coarse grass and mud. There is enough firm ground in the south-west corner, however, for an army to pitch camp. At high water the Blackwater estuary encircles the island, but at low tide Northey is an island in a sea of mud. A narrow black causeway, visible only when the water recedes,

connects the island to the south bank of the river a mile east of Maldon. One thousand years after the battle, the scene remains the same – the river, the island and the plain to the south – flat and featureless, as if the wide sky were an insupportable burden.

Most early English battles were fought hand-to-hand with wide slashing swords and spears used for both thrusting and throwing, although arrows played some part. To these weapons, the Danes added their fearsome axe.

Britnoth brought his army to the waterside and formed a close line of battle at the mouth of the causeway. The Danes sent a messenger to shout terms of surrender across the water, but Britnoth scornfully rejected this insulting offer. At low tide the causeway became passable and the Danes advanced towards the mainland only to find their passage barred by three of Britnoth's strongest warriors. Realizing that an attempt to force their way across would be bloody and demor-

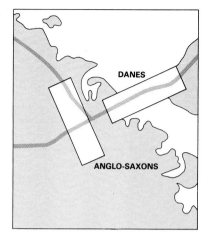

alizing, they cunningly appealed to Britnoth's sense of fair-play, asking him to let them cross to the mainland so that they could fight equally on dry land. To the childlike general of the Anglo-Saxons this seemed a perfectly reasonable request (though the poet/historian

makes it clear that such innocent gallantry was extraordinary even in those simpler days). He invited the Danes to his side of the causeway, formed his men into a defensive shield-wall and awaited the attack.

The Danes advanced remorselessly, and Britnoth was soon wounded by a spear. Flinging his own weapon back, he killed his assailant, but as he laughed in triumph, another spear caught him in the side. Then the old man swayed and fell before the Danish swords and battle-axes.

At this early setback a number of the Anglo-Saxons panicked and fled (one of them on Britnoth's own horse.) But the most loyal of Britnoth's companions, determined to see the game to its end, stayed on against now-impossible odds and fell one by one on the flat fields by the River Blackwater.

The Danes continued their coastal raids, unopposed by the people of Essex. And the body of Britnoth, his head replaced by a lump of wax, was laid to rest in Ely Cathedral.

The battlefield of Maldon lies to the east of the town along the banks of the River Blackwater. From Maldon drive towards Latchingford on the B1018. In less than a mile a paved lane on the left leads to South House Farm and the battlefield. As this is not a right of way for vehicles, leave your car on the main road and continue the journey on foot. Walk through the farmyard and follow the road out across the flat agricultural land towards the river. These are the fields where the giant Britnoth deployed his army and then shouted across to the Danes on Northey Island his overconfident invitation to join him in battle on the mainland. Here also he fell and was beheaded by the victorious Danes.

The island, where the Danes encamped, is straight ahead of you, connected to the land by a narrow black causeway. As in 991, this is passable only at low water. It is no more than twelve feet wide, but it is difficult to imagine three men defending it against an army. Northey Island is now a bird sanctuary maintained by the National Trust. It is possible to obtain permission to visit it by writing to the Resident Warden.

An alternative way of reaching the battlefield is to walk along the riverside on a path leading from the marina in Maldon. A right of way exists all around the banks of the Blackwater estuary and is one of the flattest coastal paths in Britain.

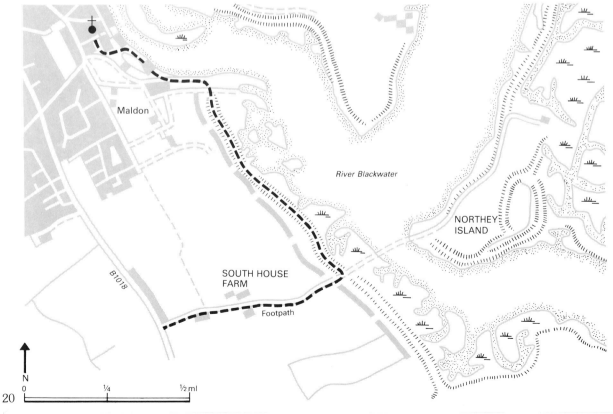

Maldon

River Blackwater

NORTHEY ISLAND

B1018

SOUTH HOUSE FARM

Footpath

N

0   ¼   ½ ml

The flat fields (above and below) to the south-west of Northey Island, along the banks of the River Blackwater. Britnoth, the Anglo-Saxon leader, brought his army to this plain in order to confront the Danes. He allowed the Danes a safe passage from Northey Island to the mainland, an act of gallantry which cost him his life.

The Battle of Ashingdon

1016 was a turbulent year in English history. *The Anglo-Saxon Chronicle,* which generally restricts itself to terse comments about political events, in that year grows quite garrulous when describing the warfare between Edmund Ironside and King Canute. The climax of their encounters was the Battle of Ashingdon.

Canute, king of the Danes, was an indefatigable campaigner. In 1016 he led expeditions to the west country, the midlands, the north and the east, plundering what he could and fighting when necessary. As the year wore on, however, he met with increasingly stiff resistance from the Anglo-Saxons, since King Ethelred had died in April and the twenty-two year-old Edmund Ironside, who succeeded him, was an energetic and popular leader. Edmund worsted Canute in several battles, but for months the wily Dane avoided complete defeat and succeeded in slipping back to his ships. Once at sea, the temptation of yet another lightning raid on the defenceless British coastline was always too great to resist.

In October Edmund finally caught up with his elusive enemies in Essex before they could reach their ships. The Danish fleet was anchored in the River Crouch. The Danes, although within sight of the water, were forced to make a stand on the hill now the site of the village of Canewdon. Less than two miles to their west, on the hill at Ashingdon, was the larger army of Edmund, confident from its recent successes and exultant at having finally trapped the enemy.

On the morning of the eighteenth of October the two armies moved down to the ridge that connected their hilltop positions, the Danes cautiously, the Anglo-Saxons impetuously. Edmund's men flung themselves into battle, and the laborious butchery of early warfare began. The slaughter may have been underway for some time before the Anglo-Saxon king noticed that not all his army was engaged. Halfway down the hillside behind him stood the force commanded by Edric, an earl who had defected to the Danes a year before and then returned to the foolishly forgiving Edmund just prior to the Ashingdon campaign.

Now the Danes, thanks to Edric's refusal to fight, found themselves with the advantage of numbers, and surrounded the desperate and demoralized English. King Edmund was one of the few who escaped. The rest were cut down in an ever-diminishing circle until at sunset the only Englishmen remaining on the field were either traitors or corpses. *"All the nobility of England was there destroyed,"* says *The Anglo-Saxon Chronicle.*

Broken in body and in spirit, Edmund died at the end of November, and the kingdom passed to Canute. Edric was appointed to rule a quarter of England, but the fruits of his villainy did not feed him long. In the following year he was killed in London and his corpse thrown over the city walls.

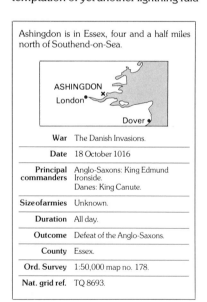

Ashingdon is in Essex, four and a half miles north of Southend-on-Sea.

War	The Danish Invasions.
Date	18 October 1016
Principal commanders	Anglo-Saxons: King Edmund Ironside. Danes: King Canute.
Size of armies	Unknown.
Duration	All day.
Outcome	Defeat of the Anglo-Saxons.
County	Essex.
Ord. Survey	1:50,000 map no. 178.
Nat. grid ref.	TQ 8693.

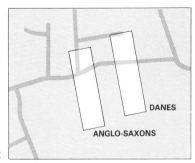

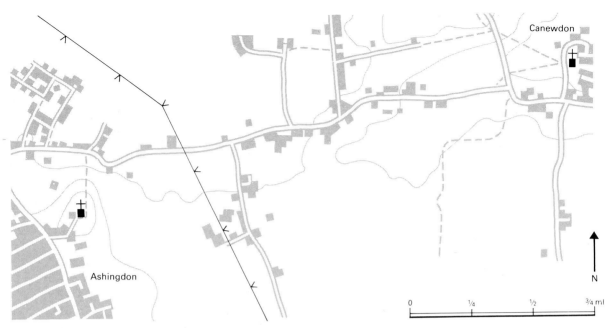

Ashingdon is not a field which repays close inspection. Too much of the area is inaccessible and much of what is written about the location of the battle is based solely upon informed (or prejudiced) speculation. But Ashingdon Church is well worth a visit, a tiny building with its origins in Saxon times and a fine view east to Canewdon – the same view that stretched before Edmund Ironside on the morning of the battle.

From Southend-on-Sea in Essex take the B1013 to Rochford and turn right at the T-junction to Ashingdon. In two miles a lane to the right leads up a hill to the church. Canewdon, where the Danes prepared for battle, is immediately visible to the east because its church, like the one at Ashingdon, is situated conspicuously on a hilltop. The River Crouch, where the Danish fleet lay anchored, is just visible across the flat land to the north. In between the hills of Ashingdon and Canewdon is a stretch of slightly higher land where the armies met. In their impetuous charge, the Anglo-Saxons may well have covered two-thirds of the distance, meeting the Danes (to their own disadvantage) at the point where the land begins to rise towards Canewdon.

The confusion which surrounds this battle is evident from the Ashingdon Church information leaflet which, although agreeing that the Anglo-Saxons occupied the site of the church, has them facing the other way in order to cut off the Danes who were returning to their ships from the west.

The churchyard at Ashingdon stands on an isolated hill over-looking the plain to the east. It is near here that Edmund Ironside compelled the Danes into battle.

The Battle of Hastings

On a low ridge six miles north of Hastings, Harold Godwinson and his army of Saxon English vainly defended an entire kingdom. It is the most famous battlefield in Britain, one of those rare spots where the events of a single day totally reversed the fortunes of a nation. Harold chose to defend, squeezing seven or eight thousand men into a single deep line less than half a mile long. William of Normandy was compelled to advance, with foot soldiers and cavalry, through a marshy depression called Senlac, then up the slope to encounter the Saxons.

The battle lasted a full day, beginning some time after nine o'clock. By twilight Harold and his two brothers lay dead, the king's body hacked to pieces at the centre of the ridge. His surviving soldiers straggled into the forest to the north, safe for a time from pursuit. They never again assembled to confront the Norman invaders.

Honouring a pre-battle pledge, William built an abbey on the centre of Senlac Ridge where Harold had fallen. Its ruins remain, reinforced by the harmonious modern buildings of Battle Abbey School. From the terrace of the school the visitor sees, as Harold once did, the open, sloping field across which William and his army of Normans, Bretons and Frenchmen inexorably advanced – first with a storm of arrows, then with horsemen, finally on foot, struggling under heavy chain mail up to the Saxon line. Farther south are the wooded hills among which the Norman army marched on their way from Hastings the morning of the battle. On Telham Hill, about a mile from Senlac Ridge, William paused to arm himself and reconnoitre. It was then that the two armies confronted each other for the first time. To Harold, the surface of the hill itself must have taken on a bristling,

menacing life. Perhaps even from that distance he could see the Papal banner flying above William's army, a discouraging sign that the Church had picked a favourite in the fight for England. Exhausted by the forced march that had brought him from Stamford Bridge in Yorkshire only a few days before, and by the preparations for yet another battle, Harold, for all his valour, must have felt singled out for divine rebuke.

From his briefly superior position on the slopes of Telham Hill, William could see the compressed Saxon line, a single mass of foot soldiers. As he descended to the valley below Harold's army and prepared to deploy his men, this formation became a formidable wall, the last barrier between himself and a kingdom.

Today the walls of the school and the abbey rise like a petrified army above Senlac Ridge. They are most

24

Sheep graze among trees on the western slopes of Senlac Ridge. It was on this side of the field, Harold's right flank, that the Bretons suffered an early setback.

Crumbling walls are all that remain of Pevensey Castle (below). This coastal stronghold, near Hastings, was William's first conquest upon landing in England.

The Battle of Hastings was fought six miles north of Hastings in East Sussex, where the A2100 and the A269 now meet at Battle.

War	The Norman Invasion.
Date	14 October 1066.
Principal commanders	Anglo-Saxons: King Harold Godwinson. Normans: William, Duke of Normandy.
Size of armies	Anglo-Saxons: About 8,000. Normans: About 9,000.
Duration	From about 9:30 a.m. until dusk.
Outcome	Defeat of the Anglo-Saxons and death of King Harold.
County	East Sussex.
Ord. Survey	1:50,000 map no 199.
Nat. grid ref.	TQ 7415.

strikingly visible from the B2095 where, as Powdermill Lane, it runs south-east of the battlefield and roughly parallel with the lines of battle. Through gaps in the hedge on the north side of the road one can see the broad field where William's left flank, mainly Bretons, and the left of his central group of Normans charged up the hill. They would have an easier time in their attack today. Since 1066 the ground has risen and the wet land below the ridge has been drained to form ponds. Armies of school children now can charge dry-footed over land where so many of William's horsemen came to grief.

This western side of the field, a tranquil parkland with scattered, broad trees, standing water and flocks of sheep, was the scene of William's only real setback in the battle. After an ineffectual attempt to weaken the Saxon line with arrows, he ordered an advance. This met with fierce resistance from the Saxons. Armed with axes, spears and even stones, they battered William's cavalry to a standstill and eventually forced the Bretons to retreat. The jubilant, undisciplined soldiers on the right flank of Harold's army set off downhill in pursuit. They closed upon the retreating enemy at the bottom of the hill but were themselves attacked as William rallied his troops. Harold and his remaining army watched their companions slaughtered in the marshy land below.

From the Abbey School grounds a modern visitor is directed on a self-guided tour of this half of the battlefield. He descends the slope, following the fatal route of Harold's impetuous right wing. Three-dimensional models of the battle take him through its various phases: the repeated Norman assaults, the false retreat which lured another section of Harold's army to its destruction, the murderously steep rain of arrows which demoralized the defenders and wounded the king. The tour ends at the abbey, where the final assault drove the last Saxons from the ridge. A monument in the abbey grounds marks the spot where Harold fell, blinded by an arrow in the eye. Dismembered and disembowelled, he was unidentifiable among the corpses of his house carls.

William the Conqueror, a man who believed in doing things properly, was crowned on Christmas day, more than two months after his victory, but he could have proclaimed himself king on the spot. "It was," wrote William of Malmesbury in the next century, "as if the whole strength of England had fallen with Harold."

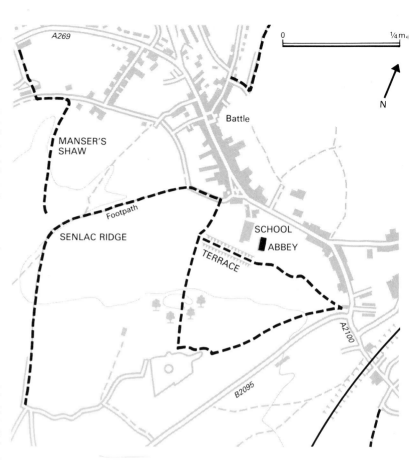

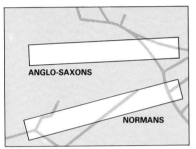

Ponds have been created in the western part of the battlefield, where marshy land once impeded the advance of Bretons on William's left flank. Harold's soldiers, pursuing the Bretons across this ground, themselves became enmired.

Senlac Ridge (below) as it appears from Powdermill Lane near the centre of the battlefield. Harold's position is now occupied by the ruined abbey and Battle Abbey School.

Battle is a small town, still dominated by the events of 1066, so the grounds of Battle Abbey School, scene of much of the fighting, are the chief tourist attraction. These provide the best view of the western side of the battlefield of Hastings. A circular walk of about a mile leads the visitor down beside the recently-created ponds and along the Norman line before returning up through the ruined abbey itself to Harold's monument. The school terrace is the best place from which to appreciate fully Harold's formidable position. This tour is enhanced by several admirable battle information panels which tell the story chronologically.

A longer circuit, leading from the car park, skirts the outside boundary of the school grounds among park and pasture-land down to Powdermill Lane (the B2095). From here there is a splendid Norman's-eye-view of the Saxon position on Senlac Ridge, now the site of the school and the abbey.

Just a mile south-east of the battlefield is Telham Hill, where William and his men stopped to arm themselves on the morning of the battle. From the summit one looks down on Senlac Ridge and the town of Battle 100 feet below. For a pleasant cross-country walk, take the track that leads south off the A2100 immediately east of the railway bridge. William's army advanced down this slope shortly after daybreak on the morning of the fourteenth of October. A secondary road at the top descends westwards to Powdermill Lane.

Harold's position on the east side of the battlefield is largely obscured by the buildings of Marley Lane. Caldbec Hill, the Saxon look-out point half a mile behind the battle line, is on the B2092 which, as Mount Street, leads off the High Street. A modern windmill marks the place where Harold's exhausted army may have gathered on the eve of the battle.

200 yards farther along Mount Street, a track leads right down the slopes of Caldbec Hill to farmland that is criss-crossed with public rights of way. This area lies directly behind Harold's left flank and must have witnessed the rout of the shattered Saxon army as they fled to the woods.

At the bottom of the recreation ground, just off the A269, is a steep, wooded gully called Manser's Shaw. Legend has it that this is Malfosse, where Norman horsemen plunged to a savage death at the hands of the retreating Saxons.

The grounds of Battle Abbey School are open weekdays 9-1, 2-5 (or dusk); Saturday until 12:45; all day Saturday and Sunday 1 August to 15 September.

Battle Museum, facing the abbey gateway, has a diorama of the battle and a reproduction of the Bayeux Tapestry, the world's most famous embroidery. It is open Easter to early October, weekdays 10-1, 2-5; Sunday 2:30-5.30.

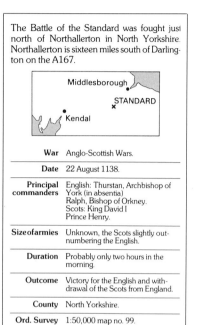

The Battle of the Standard was fought just north of Northallerton in North Yorkshire. Northallerton is sixteen miles south of Darlington on the A167.

War	Anglo-Scottish Wars.
Date	22 August 1138.
Principal commanders	English: Thurstan, Archbishop of York (in absentia) Ralph, Bishop of Orkney. Scots: King David I Prince Henry.
Size of armies	Unknown, the Scots slightly outnumbering the English.
Duration	Probably only two hours in the morning.
Outcome	Victory for the English and withdrawal of the Scots from England.
County	North Yorkshire.
Ord. Survey	1:50,000 map no. 99.
Nat. grid ref.	SE 3697.

Standard Hill Farm is situated on a slight rise to the south of the battlefield. It is near here that the army of Archbishop Thurston awaited the Scottish attack.

The Battle of the Standard

On Cowton Moor in 1138 the Christian church won a major military victory. An aged archbishop inspired the English campaign; priests served as recruiting officers; and the army rallied on the moor around the banners of saints and a vessel containing communion bread.

The battle that ensued was a major conflict in the struggle for the English crown between King Stephen and the Empress Matilda, his cousin. Matilda, daughter of King Henry I, had a strong claim to the throne. Her interests were represented by her uncle, David I of Scotland, who saw in England's confusion an opportunity to annex Northumberland while appearing to be of service to his niece. King Stephen, embroiled in rebellion in the south, had no obvious hero to defend his northern kingdom until Thurstan, Archbishop of

York, rallied the church army. Thurstan issued a proclamation, which made it clear that to take arms against the Scots would be a short-cut to salvation, while not to do so would result in eternal discomfort. Led by their priests, his devout recruits assembled at York. The old Archbishop longed to join them in their march north but he was bedridden and sent in his stead the Bishop of Orkney as spiritual general.

On the morning of the twenty-second of August, Thurstan's army faced the Scots on moorland three miles north of Northallerton. Rising above the centre of their line, within sight of their puzzled enemy, was a ship's mast mounted on a cart and hung with banners of the four Yorkshire saints. On top of this colourful standard was a pyx, a communion vessel containing the host.

The battle was a short one. The unarmoured Scots from Galloway, who had insisted on leading the attack, were repulsed by a cloud of English arrows until they were, according to a contemporary, *"covered with spines like a hedgehog"*. Prince Henry, on the Scottish right flank, broke through the English line in a fierce charge, but he was surrounded and barely escaped with his life. The retreating Scots were slaughtered by the thousands on the land now known as Standard Hill.

No battlefield creates a more peaceful scene than Standard Hill today. Two farms and quiet fields of grain occupy the centre of the action. Heather, which is said never to grow over Scottish dead, is entirely absent.

"It grows good wheat," said Mrs Lily Jamieson of Standard Hill Farm, *"in spite of a lot of clay."*

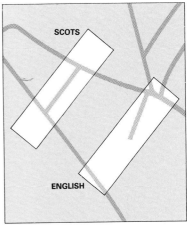

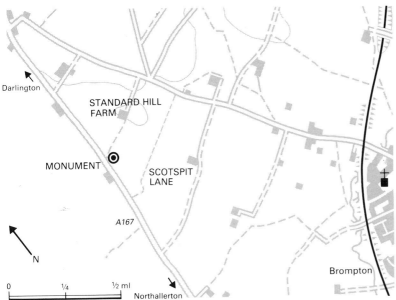

The monument to the Battle of the Standard is on the A167, nearly three miles north of Northallerton, on the right as you drive towards Darlington. It is a rather truncated obelisk that appears to be much favoured as a roosting place by local birds. It marks a point just behind the left flank of the English line, but since the traffic on this road is remorseless, it is wiser to inspect the field from the east. Continue along the A167 for 1,000 yards, then turn right on a secondary road to Brompton. In a quarter of a mile you pass a neat cluster of farm buildings on a low rise to the right. This is very likely the place where the Scots drew up and, looking south, first saw the tall standard that so inspired the English.

Continue along this road for another quarter mile. The fields of grain to your right now replace the once bloody moorland. Standard Hill Farm, also on the right of the road, faces south, away from the field of battle. It too occupies a low hill, the centre of the English line and the spot where the standard itself may well have flown.

Another 200 yards towards Brompton brings you to Scotspit Lane, a completely overgrown avenue of oaks and chestnuts. According to legend, the burial pits of 10,000 Scots lie along this ancient track. It is possible to reach the A167 Northallerton road by walking along Scotspit Lane, and thus traverse the south of the field, but mud in winter and neck-high nettles in summer make this an unpleasant hike.

The Battle of Lewes

The city of Lewes has grown since the fourteenth of May 1264, but not to an unrecognizable extent. The River Ouse still crawls through flat pastureland to the north and south, and the downs rise abruptly on either side, as uncluttered today as when Simon de Montfort assembled his army on Offham Hill, just north-west of the city. Then as now, the keep of Lewes Castle dominated the skyline, though Simon saw it only as a modern and efficient fortification, where Edward, the king's son, prepared for battle. King Henry III himself was in Lewes, staying at the priory half a mile from his son. His royal army was full of confidence. They had waged a successful campaign against the rebellious barons and, in the previous few months, had taken Northampton, Leicester, Nottingham, Rochester and Tonbridge. Now, facing an army of little more than 5,000 men, they anticipated crushing both the rebellion and its leader in one encounter.

The king knew his opponent as well as he knew any man. Simon de Mont-

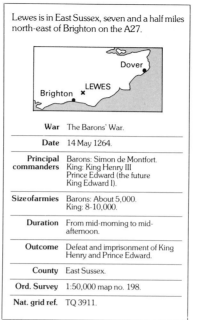

Lewes is in East Sussex, seven and a half miles north-east of Brighton on the A27.

War	The Barons' War.
Date	14 May 1264.
Principal commanders	Barons: Simon de Montfort. King: King Henry III Prince Edward (the future King Edward I).
Size of armies	Barons: About 5,000. King: 8-10,000.
Duration	From mid-morning to mid-afternoon.
Outcome	Defeat and imprisonment of King Henry and Prince Edward.
County	East Sussex.
Ord. Survey	1:50,000 map no. 198.
Nat. grid ref.	TQ 3911.

fort was married to Henry's sister and for years had been his chief general and closest adviser. Well into his sixties, he was still an inspiring leader, but his army was dwindling and his allies were having second thoughts. Lewes itself had recently been handed over to the king by John de Warenne, Earl of Surrey, a former friend of Simon's.

Although both the king and his son expected a battle, neither was totally prepared for the speed at which Simon went to work. At daybreak on the fourteenth of May, the rebel army was eight miles north of Lewes, still at camp in the village of Fletching. By mid-morning they had prepared for battle in an ideal position, spreading themselves out on a long, flat ridge overlooking the city. So rapid was their approach that they even captured Henry's sentry — literally napping, according to one early account.

This splendid plateau is now partly cultivated but still provides the visitor with an excellent chance to examine Simon's position. The deep chalk track

The windswept western slopes of the battlefield at Lewes are today a training gallop for race horses. This is an appropriate use of the land, as it was here that Simon's downhill charge vanquished King Henry.

that leads up the hill south-west of the village of Offham is very likely that chosen by the rebel army to gain an advantageous position quickly and inconspicuously. Had they advanced directly to Lewes they would have found themselves on the route of the present-day A275, squeezed between a precipitous hillside and a marshy river valley. A few of Simon's men might even have found time to enjoy the view. Behind them rose Mt. Harry, a prelude to miles of downland; to the left, the River Ouse, meandering self-indulgently on a rich plain 300 feet below. Directly in front of them lay Lewes, dwarfed by more downland that sheered up behind it as if to cut off its retreat.

Prince Edward in Lewes Castle was the first to discover Simon's proximity. As if to live up to a reputation of being a headstrong youth, he immediately mounted and charged up the long hill with his cavalry, not giving the poor king, his father, a chance to assemble his forces. Edward was spectacularly

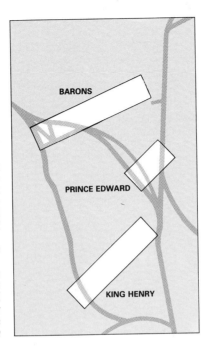

successful. He routed the left flank of Simon's army, a band of inexperienced Londoners stationed where the chalk pits are now, and drove them down the steep hill which they had climbed only an hour or two earlier. Rashly, he then continued the pursuit until the battle was far behind.

When King Henry finally reached the field he found to his dismay that his son had disappeared, leaving him to fight it out with his brother-in-law. All along the lower slopes of the field down to where a housing estate juts into the farmland, King Henry took a battering. He himself *"was much beaten with swords and maces"*. His brother, Prince Richard, was ignominiously trapped in a windmill. By the time the exuberant Prince Edward returned, the battle was lost.

"King Simon" was never crowned, but for fifteen months he ruled England, establishing during his brief reign the first elected parliament. The following year, at the Battle of Evesham, he paid for his principles with his life.

The battlefield of Lewes is partly built on today, but enough of it is open land to make it a rewarding site to visit. Offham Hill, where Simon de Montfort deployed his troops, is a mile north-west of the centre of Lewes. It can be reached by a steep path leading off the A275, just opposite Offham Church, or by a road up the gentler north slope from Lewes. The first route is likely to be that taken by Simon's army. Where the path starts to level off, turn left to reach the position of Simon's left flank in about 200 yards. Here is where Prince Edward drove back the Londoners in the first stage of the battle. An energetic tourist may well be tempted to discover a distant view of Lewes from Mt. Harry. To reach the summit (640 ft.) continue along the same track from Offham Hill. In wet weather be prepared to carry several pounds of chalky mud on your boots. The view in both directions is ample compensation.

Just north of Wallands Park, a modern housing estate, are tracks which lead off the A275 to the old race course buildings, the area where Simon established his right flank. Down the hill from here, along a training gallop for race horses, is the approximate path of Simon's own cavalry charge, which finally broke the king's diminished army. A modern prison now impedes the route of Henry's retreat. Lewes Castle, where Prince Edward stayed on the eve of the battle, provides another fine view of the battlefield. It is open weekdays 10-5; Sundays (April to October) 2-5.

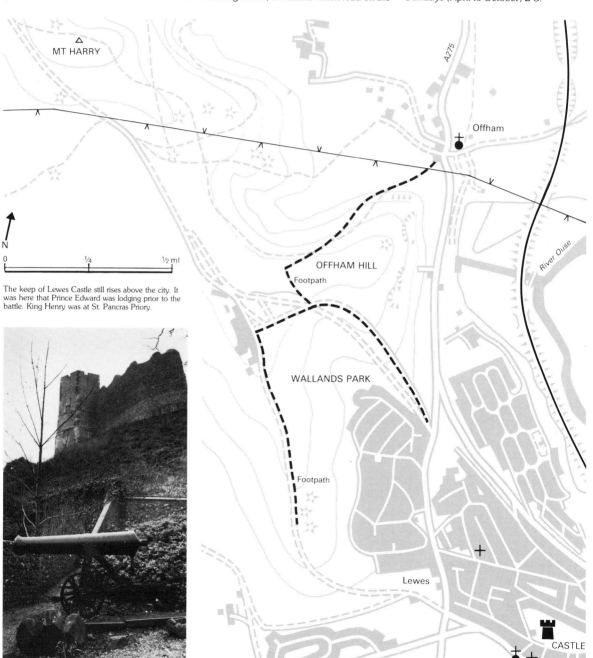

The keep of Lewes Castle still rises above the city. It was here that Prince Edward was lodging prior to the battle. King Henry was at St. Pancras Priory.

The long slope of Offham Hill as seen from the south (above). It was this view that confronted King Henry when he arrived at the field. His son, Prince Edward, had already attacked.

The hill on which Lewes Castle is situated commands a fine view (given clear weather) of Simon's position. Simon nevertheless took Henry by surprise.

The Siege and Storming of Kildrummy Castle

On the twenty-fifth of March 1306 Robert Bruce was crowned King Robert I of Scotland. This was as much a capricious act of wishfulfilment on Bruce's part as a popularly sanctioned coronation. Just six weeks before the ceremony he had murdered his nearest rival, John Comyn, in front of the high altar in the Greyfriars' church at Dumfries. As a result the noble houses of Scotland were in disarray, while from the south came the army of Edward I with orders to suppress the rebellion mercilessly.

Within three months of his coronation, Bruce was on the run. On the nineteenth of June his men were surprised and defeated at Methven by an English army commanded by Aymer de Valence. A few weeks later his disillusioned soldiers scattered at Dalry before John Macdougall, a Scottish enemy. Bruce fled to the highlands with a small band of followers. Realizing, however, that the life of an outlaw did not befit a queen, he entrusted his wife, his daughter and several other ladies to the care of his brother Neil, and instructed them to seek safety within his castle at Kildrummy.

Kildrummy Castle, then only fifty years old, was one of the most modern fortifications in Scotland. It stood on a low hill guarding a strategic pass, the main route between the land of Mar in the south and the province of Morayland in the north. The north and west sides of the castle were naturally defended by a steep ravine called Back Den. To the south and east the land sloped gently towards the high road. From without it was a formidable structure. A great ditch, up to eighty feet wide and twenty feet deep, encircled the massive curtain walls. Six round towers, dominated by the gatehouse and a donjon, completed the external defenses. But within this austere fortress was accommodation fit for a queen. Living quarters centred around a splendid hall complete with minstrel gallery, while the chapel, which had been painstakingly aligned to face east, was a surprisingly elegant work of ecclesiastical architecture to gaze from such a warlike facade.

The queen and her ladies did not stay long at Kildrummy. When news came that the young Prince of Wales (soon to be Edward II) and Aymer de Valence were preparing to besiege the castle, they travelled north to the supposed safety of Tain (where they were taken and led into years of cruel captivity in England). At first it seemed as though their journey had been needless. The garrison at the castle was well supplied with food and water and staged a dogged defence against the best siege engineers in England. On several occasions they launched devastating sorties down the hill to the south, so demoralizing the English that they seriously began to consider withdrawing from this siege which promised to drag on into the winter.

Kildrummy, like Troy, was finally taken by guile. The English discovered a fatal weakness in the castle's defence, not in the stone but in the corrupt spirit of Osborne, the Scottish blacksmith. Seduced by the promise of all the gold he could carry, Osborne seized a red hot iron from his fire and threw it in a huge pile of grain that lay in a storeroom directly beneath the great hall. In an instant the residential quarters were

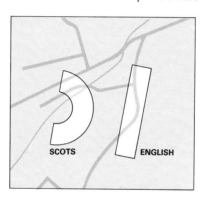

ablaze, and the terrified defenders crowded on to the walls to escape the heat. Here they were trapped between the flames within and the attacking English army without. The gate itself fell in the blaze, but the heat was so intense that it kept the English from breaking into the courtyard. Before daybreak the Scots had re-erected their defences at the gatehouse, but now they were in no position to prolong the siege. They had neither food nor water nor shelter. Kildrummy Castle had become their prison.

The English showed no mercy. Sir Neil Bruce was hanged, drawn and beheaded. His soldiers underwent less ceremonious deaths (generally the beheading was omitted). Osborne, the traitor, took his reward to the grave; "all the gold he could carry" was poured molten down his throat.

Kildrummy Castle is in the Grampian Region of Scotland on the A97, sixteen miles south of Huntly.

War	The Wars of Scottish Independence.
Date	Early September 1306.
Principal commanders	English: Edward Prince of Wales Aymer de Valence. Scots: Sir Neil Bruce.
Size of armies	Unknown.
Duration	Unknown.
Outcome	Capture of the castle. Execution of Bruce and many of his followers.
County	Grampian Region (Scotland).
Ord. Survey	1:50,000 map no. 37.
Nat. grid ref.	NJ 4516.

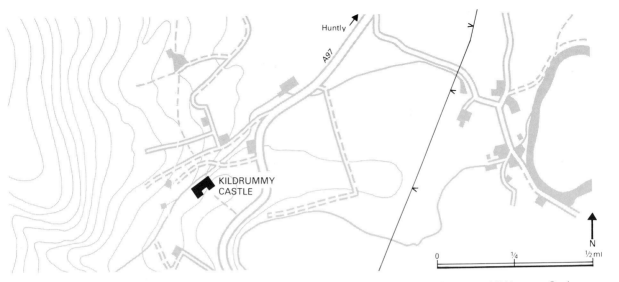

KILDRUMMY
CASTLE

Huntly

A97

N

0   ¼   ½ ml

Only the ruins of Kildrummy Castle now watch over the pass to Morayland. They stand on a hill 200 yards to the west of the A97, sixteen miles south of Huntly in the Grampian Region of Scotland. The castle was rebuilt after the siege of 1306 and for four centuries remained one of Scotland's most important fortresses, the seat of the Earls of Mar. After the failure of the Jacobite Rebellion of 1715 the castle fell into disrepair, crumbling before the predatory local builders, who saw it only as a cheap source of ready-cut stone. By the time Queen Victoria picnicked within its walls in 1866 it was a picturesque ruin, and so it remains today, a jagged shell of stone set in an immaculately trimmed lawn.

The path from the car park leads up through fields, now farmland, where the English army and Scottish defenders clashed in fierce, inconclusive skirmishes during the siege. Of the building itself, the gatehouse, most convenient to the road for eighteenth-century stone merchants, is nearly entirely flattened, but the elegant chapel window stands high on the east wall. Behind it is the rectangular outline of the great hall. This is doubtless the basement level where the pile of grain burst into flames in 1306 and quickly ignited the floorboards of the hall above.

The castle is maintained by the Department of the Environment and is officially open April to September, weekdays 9:30-7, Sunday 2-7; October to March, weekdays 9:30-4, Sunday 2-4.

A useful guide book is available at the ticket office.

The foundations of the great hall now enclose a neatly trimmed lawn. In 1306 this was where Osborne the blacksmith, bribed by the English, started his ruinous fire. The chapel is in the background.

The Battle of Brander

The mountains in the district of Lorne in Argyllshire rise up so precipitously that they force the waters of Loch Awe into a deep ravine which is called the Pass of Brander. This long arm of the loch grows increasingly narrow, begins to flow, and finally, as the River Awe, races to the salt waters of Loch Etive near the village of Taynuilt.

In the fourteenth century the Pass of Brander was a daunting route for anyone unsure of his welcome at the far end. The cliffs to the south provide foothold for neither man nor horse. To the north the slopes rise steeply to Ben Cruachan, leaving only a meagre ribbon of level land between the water and the mountainside. Today this passage is wide enough for a paved road. In 1309 it was the only route for the army of Robert Bruce on his expedition to subdue the intransigent Macdougalls of Argyllshire.

In two years Bruce had emerged from a fugitive life in the Highlands to a position where nearly all of Scotland acknowledged him as King Robert I. Two notable exceptions holding out were Alexander Macdougall and his son John Bacach, known as John of Lorne. Old Alexander had never forgiven Bruce for murdering his nephew John Comyn. When it became clear that Bruce was about to march into their territory through the Pass of Brander, John of Lorne welcomed the opportunity to avenge his cousin's death. Although his 2,000 men were outnumbered by Bruce's army, he was defending one of the most impregnable passes in Scotland. To make doubly sure of victory he placed his men part way up the rough slopes of Ben Cruachan, intending to ambush Bruce as his army straggled through the ravine below.

Well-acquainted with mountain warfare, Bruce anticipated such tactics. He divided his army in two, sending a group of archers under James Douglas up the slopes of the mountain out of sight of the enemy, while he himself continued his slow progress along the track. The Macdougalls, believing Bruce's entire army to be at their mercy, began a furious attack, rolling huge boulders down upon the advancing column. Far from panicking, their opponents scrambled up the hill to meet them on an equal footing. Then from high up the mountain came a silent shower of arrows as Douglas's men appeared on the slopes of Ben Cruachan, firing into the helpless mass of men below. John of Lorne's army, so confident just minutes before, now broke and fled, making for the River Awe and the bridge, which was their only safe crossing. They intended to seal off their retreat by destroying the bridge, but Bruce's army was too swift for them. In the flat field on the far bank and in the widening valley all the way to the sea, corpses of the Clan Macdougall marked a path to the heart of Argyllshire.

John of Lorne, ostensibly the Macdougall commander, had spent the duration of the battle in a boat on Loch Etive. When word came of the unexpected outcome, he was in an admirable position to escape. For the remaining eight years of his life he was a faithful servant of Edward III, continuing to wage war against Bruce and his allies, men to whom he stubbornly referred to as *"the Scottish rebels"*.

The Pass of Brander lies along the A85 in the Strathclyde Region of Scotland. It is fourteen miles by road east of Oban.

War	The Wars of Scottish Independence.
Date	Late summer 1309.
Principal commanders	King's army: Robert Bruce (King Robert I). Macdougalls: John of Lorne.
Size of armies	The Macdougalls, with about 2,000 men, were outnumbered by Bruce's army.
Duration	Unknown.
Outcome	Defeat of the Macdougalls.
County	Strathclyde Region (Scotland).
Ord. Survey	1:50,000 map no. 50.
Nat. grid ref.	NN 0428.

The River Awe was a formidable barrier to the fleeing Macdougalls. Many of those who managed to struggle across met their deaths on the opposite bank.

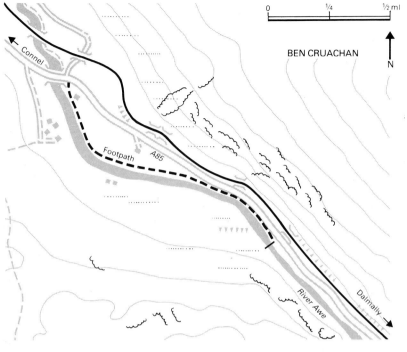

BEN CRUACHAN

N

Connel

Footpath   A85

River Awe

Dalmally

Today Robert Bruce could transport his army through the Pass of Brander either by rail or by road. The A85 and the railway run side-by-side into what was once the nearly inaccessible homeland of the Macdougalls. From the town of Dalmally on the A85 drive west towards Connel. In about three miles you pass through the village of Lochawe, claimed to be the point at which Bruce despatched James Douglas and a party of soldiers in order to outflank the awaiting Macdougalls. Since the field of battle was still several miles away, Bruce seems to have put Douglas to an unnecessary amount of hill walking. The extraordinary neo-Norman church at Lochawe has a romantic monument to Bruce.

Continue along the A85. The steep slopes to your right lead up to Ben Cruachan (3,689 ft.). To your left is the River Awe, which narrows into a torrent as it approaches the sea.

About nine miles west of Dalmally the pass begins to open up where a barrage partially obstructs the flow of the River Awe. The pasture across the river is, according to local tradition, the battlefield itself. Tumble-down cairns near the water are believed to mark graves of the Macdougall dead. This

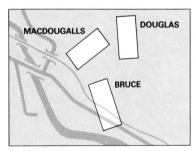

MACDOUGALLS   DOUGLAS

BRUCE

field is quite likely a scene of the bloody aftermath rather than of the battle itself. The initial stages occurred to the north of the river, probably near the point of the modern bridge, a mile beyond the barrage, where the slopes of Ben Cruachan level out enough to have permitted John of Lorne's army to wait in ambush for Bruce. The exact site of the ancient bridge over which Lorne's army retreated in panic is unknown, but his men must have spilled into the field on the south side and put up a desperate resistance. Many would not have passed over the bridge at all but would have attempted the perilous crossing on foot.

If you leave your car at the barrage and follow the little path along the river bank, you can appreciate the barrier that these rapids presented to the fleeing Mac-dougalls. Many who survived the waters fell to the sword; their graves lie just above you on the opposite bank.

The Battle of Halidon Hill

On the twenty-fourth of March 1333 Richard the Goldsmith of Cowick in Yorkshire received an urgent commission to construct two siege engines. Twenty-four oxen hauled the wood of forty oaks to Cowick Manor where, under Richard's supervision, a small army of ropers, smiths and carpenters put these huge machines together. Simultaneously six quarrymen and thirty-seven stone masons were employed to produce tons of massive stone shot. At the end of May the siege engines arrived by ship at Berwick in Northumberland, where the armies of King Edward III and Edward Balliol, the puppet "king" of Scotland, had determined that if they could not break the will of the Scottish defenders, they could most certainly break their walls.

Edward III's intentions in besieging Berwick were twofold: he wished to capture this strategically important Scottish city; he also wished to draw a large Scottish army into open battle, an engagement he was confident of winning. As obsessed with subduing the Scots as had been his grandfather Edward I, the king was galled that only a few of the Scottish nobles rallied around his choice of king, Edward Balliol. The rest adhered to Robert Bruce's nine-year-old son King David II, whose guardian, Archibald Douglas, grew increasingly bold in his sorties across the border.

The siege was severe, and although the citizens of Berwick defended themselves resolutely, they were hammered by missiles from the land and harrassed by the English fleet from the sea. At last they appealed for a truce and received what must have seemed generous terms from King Edward: if in four days a Scottish army had not defeated the English or had not, at least, succeeded in breaking through the English defences and entering the city with 200 men, then Berwick would surrender. This seemed to give the Scots every opportunity of victory, for Sir Archibald Douglas and a large army had for some time been raiding the neighbouring countryside in an attempt to draw off the besieging army. The inhabitants of Berwick were even allowed to inform Douglas of the terms of truce. On the morning of the nineteenth of July, just one day before the deadline for the surrender of Berwick, the Scots drew up three miles north-west of the city. In front of them was Halidon Hill and the English army.

At this point it may have been apparent to the Scottish leaders that their task was not as simple as it had seemed on paper. In Halidon Hill the English had found a strong position, which they were obliged by the terms of the treaty to do nothing but defend until vespers of that day. On the slopes of Witches' Knowe, a hill to the north of Edward's army, the Scots were also well-placed for a defensive battle, but they had committed themselves to attack and before them lay an unwelcoming area of boggy land, which would render their horses useless. They waited until midday, when the tide was high enough in the River Tweed to deny the English any means of retreating, then prepared to advance – on foot, up hill and through a treacherous marsh.

Before the Scots began their attack, a macabre incident occurred. A massive man called Turnbull (because he had saved Robert Bruce from a wild bull), stepped out from the Scottish army, accompanied by a mastiff, and challenged any Englishman to single combat. The soldier who emerged from the army on Halidon Hill, though of average height, was more than a match for both the Scotsman and his dog. He chopped the hind legs off the charging mastiff and, avoiding Turnbull's ponderous strokes, removed first the giant's left arm and then his head.

With this inauspicious single combat still in their minds, the Scots began their laborious advance into a rain of arrows. Hundreds fell before the breathless and dispirited men reached the English on Halidon Hill. There they met with a fresh and confident enemy. The Scots fought desperately but when their right flank broke before the troops of Edward Balliol, the remainder of the line was forced into a disorderly retreat. The Scottish grooms, attending their masters' horses on Witches' Knowe a mile to the north, witnessed this disaster and rode off in panic, leaving the floundering knights to an almost certain death. The pursuit lasted until nightfall and continued for miles. Scottish historians estimated that 10,000 Scots had died; English historians could find fewer than twenty casualties on their side.

King Edward III had won a wargame of his own devising. On the twentieth of July he accepted his prize by riding through the gates of Berwick. And the wars with Scotland continued, as if nothing had happened.

The view north-west from Halidon Hill (right). It was from this direction that the army of Sir Archibald Douglas advanced in 1333.

Halidon Hill is in Northumberland, two miles north-west of Berwick-upon-Tweed.

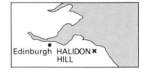

Edinburgh HALIDON HILL

War	The Wars of Scottish Independence.
Date	19 July 1333.
Principal commanders	English: King Edward III Edward Balliol. Scots: Sir Archibald Douglas.
Size of armies	Unknown, the Scots probably outnumbering the English.
Duration	From midday until dusk.
Outcome	Rout of the Scots and death of Douglas.
County	Northumberland.
Ord. Survey	1:50,000 map no. 75.
Nat. grid ref.	NU 9655.

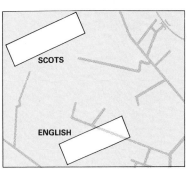

The long, gradual slope of Halidon Hill (left) proved a demoralizing obstacle to the Scottish army.

Witches' Knowe (above) from which the Scots made their ill-fated attack upon Halidon Hill. Because of boggy ground they dismounted and advanced on foot. The grooms on Witches' Knowe later panicked and escaped with the horses.

The River Tweed at Berwick Castle (below) is a major obstacle, especially at high tide. The Scots, attacking the English on Halidon Hill, waited until high water before they advanced, thus making a retreat for their enemy extremely hazardous.

Halidon Hill was a natural position for Edward to choose to defend. It rises two miles north-west of Berwick and commands long views in all directions except to the north, where Witches' Knowe, the initial Scottish position, stands in the way.

Take the A6105 towards Duns west out of Berwick. In just over a mile turn right on a secondary road. You are now climbing the east slope of Halidon Hill. In a quarter mile turn left on an unpaved farm track. This is marked "Halidon Hill, Site of Battle 1333", but there is no subsequent indication of what is to be seen. Continue along this track for nearly a mile. You are now on the north slope of Halidon Hill. The ridge diagonally ahead of you to the right is Witches' Knowe, from which the Scottish grooms watched in dismay as their army retreated in disorder. Leave the car and walk up a farm track to your left (unmarked on O.S. map no. 75). This track will not take you to the summit of Halidon Hill, which is under cultivation, but does provide a fine view of Witches' Knowe and the long, low fields over which the Scottish army advanced. There are two farms on the flat land to the north of Halidon Hill. The one to the right as you face Witches' Knowe is called Bogend, a reminder of the marsh that impeded the Scottish attack. Where you are standing on the west slope of Halidon Hill is where Edward Balliol forced back the Scottish right wing.

A neglected battle stone stands in a shaggy hedge on the north side of the A6105, about three-quarters of a mile to the west of the turn-off for Halidon Hill.

The ruins of Berwick Castle, begun in the days of Edward I, stand above the Tweed very near the railway station. They provide a magnificent view of the river and the land to the south and west. It was from the walls of this castle that the sister-in-law of Robert Bruce was hung in an open cage.

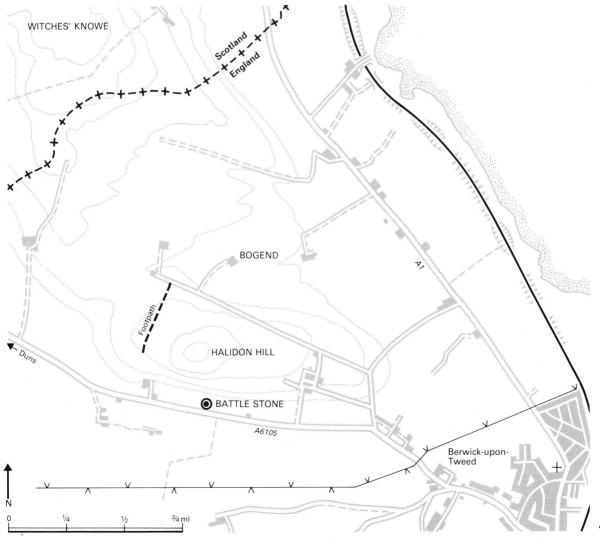

A view from Douglas's position south-east across the centre of the battlefield. West Townhead Farm is among the trees in the distance.

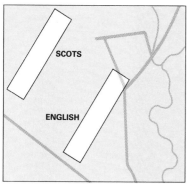

The Battle of Otterburn

Otterburn is a small town in Northumberland, thirty-two miles north-west of Newcastle.

War	The Wars of Scottish Independence.
Date	August 1388.
Principal commanders	English: Sir Henry Percy (Hotspur). Scots: James, Earl of Douglas.
Size of armies	English: About 7,000. Scots: Unknown, but smaller.
Duration	From early evening through the night.
Outcome	Defeat of the English and capture of Henry Percy. Douglas killed.
County	Northumberland.
Ord. Survey	1:50,000 map no. 80.
Nat. grid ref.	NY 8793.

The moon was nearly full in the third week of August 1388. It was the only light to fall on the field near the Otter Burn when Henry Percy and James Douglas fought their long and meaningless battle.

To both men war was a way of life – the inevitable conclusion to a quarrel, a logical solution to political problems, a glamorous way of acquiring wealth, at times almost a recreation. So it was no wonder that when Douglas, taking advantage of England's weak young King Richard II, led a small expeditionary force into Durham and Northumberland, he should have engaged in a skirmish and slanging match with the Percys, his family's arch-rivals, outside the walls of Newcastle. Young Henry Percy, known as Hotspur, was enraged when Douglas captured his pennon in one such fracas, but he was afraid that a larger Scottish force waited nearby, and did not risk his entire army in a pitched battle. Douglas, his column

swollen with the fruits of his southern adventure, turned towards Scotland along the valley of the River Rede. Whether or not he had taunted Percy as in the lines of an old ballad –

"Yet I will stay at Otterbourne,
Where you shall welcome be" –

he did wait on high ground just west of where the Otter Burn tumbles down to meet the River Rede.

Percy, realizing that in fact he outnumbered Douglas, rushed after him and discovered the Scots preparing for the night in a line across the pass. Without regard to the approaching dark, Percy charged headlong at his enemy, while sending one of his generals, possibly Sir Thomas Umfraville, on a long outflanking manoeuvre to the right.

The Scots, despite their inferior numbers, held their own. In this they were aided by the failure of Umfraville to join the battle after he had attacked their near-deserted camp from the

The Battle of Otterburn was fought on the slopes to the north-west of the village. By good fortune a public footpath bisects the area. This does not offer any especial insight into the tactics of the engagement (contemporary accounts are too vague to allow us to say exactly where the action took place) but it does provide a beautiful view of the hills that fringe the Cheviots. If a battle had not been fought on this field we would have had to invent one.

Driving west through the village of Otterburn on the A696, turn right on a secondary road to Otterburn Camp. In 200 yards stop at West Townhead Farm, the last building on the left. Walk through the farmyard and out across the fields along a track (overgrown in summer; muddy in winter). In a

A view south across the field where Douglas is supposed to have fallen. He requested that his body be concealed so that his men would not learn of his death.

quarter mile you are in the area where most of the fighting took place. Behind you, on the route you have just taken, are the fields over which the English advanced. Ahead the land slopes upwards to the high ground occupied by Douglas's left flank. His army probably stretched down to the road so as to obstruct completely Percy's route. Tradition has it that Douglas fell on the slope to your left, somewhere between where you are standing and the A696. There is no longer any "bracken-bush" under which to hide a corpse.

A little plantation down by the A696 conceals the weathered battle monument.

rear. Night fell and the action became confused. At some point in the thick of the battle Douglas was mortally wounded. An attractive Scottish legend tells how he asked to be concealed in the undergrowth so that his men would not become dispirited by knowledge of his death. Henry Percy and his brother Ralph were captured. By dawn the English had lost their zest for battle and were trickling back towards Newcastle, leaving behind them nearly 2,000 dead.

Such is the beauty of the field at Otterburn that it is best to forgo authenticity and visit the site in daylight. The hills rise exuberantly on both sides of the valley, their sides patched with plantations and flecked with sheep. Even the busy A696, which crosses the Cheviots on its way to the border country (the route of Douglas's army) is dwarfed by its surroundings. The glamorous reputation that has always accompanied the Battle of Otterburn may be more a reflection of the land itself than of deeds done there long ago.

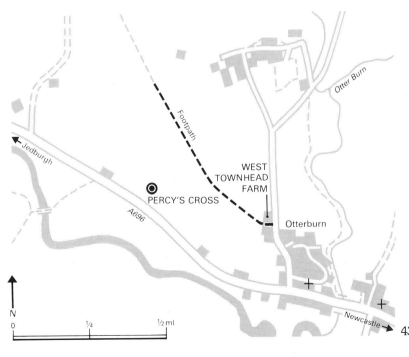

The Battle of Pilleth

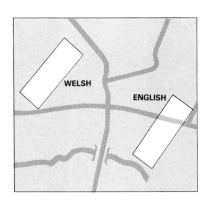

Pilleth is a tiny hamlet in Powys, five miles north-west of Presteigne on the B4356.

War	Rebellion of Owen Glendower.
Date	June 1402.
Principal commanders	English: Sir Edmund Mortimer. Welsh: Owen Glendower.
Size of armies	Unknown.
Duration	Unknown.
Outcome	Defeat of the English and capture of Mortimer.
County	Powys (Wales).
Ord. Survey	1:50,000 map no. 137.
Nat. grid ref.	SO 2568.

In the spring of the year 1402 a great comet was seen in the skies above Europe. Wherever it appeared men felt compelled to attribute to it some divine prophecy. To the northern Italians it foretold the death of the warlike Duke of Milan. To the Welsh it heralded the re-emergence of a great British nation and the defeat of the Saxons. The man chosen to lead his people in fulfilling this prophecy was Owen Glendower.

Glendower (Owain ab Gruffydd of Glyndwr) was already a threat to King Henry IV when the comet appeared. From an unremarkable youth as a law student in London and a conservative early manhood as a soldier and a landowner, he gradually became politicized, first as a supporter of Henry of Lancaster (later Henry IV) then as a champion of the Welsh people. By 1400, in his early forties, he was starting a new career in guerilla-type warfare, rarely risking a pitched battle against the English, and often disappearing into the mountains for weeks at a time. Perhaps the comet encouraged him, for in June 1402 he met the army of Sir Edmund Mortimer on the open slopes of Bryn Glas near Pilleth.

To the traveller driving west along the B4356 in Powys, Bryn Glas is a splendid sight. It steep eastern slope rises straight up from the road, a dark swathe of close-cropped grass. In the centre of this precipitous field is a rectangle of rough ground in which four tall pine trees grow. It is a conspicuous

The hilly land to the west of Pilleth (below) was ideal terrain for the guerilla campaigns of Owen Glendower.

plot, which appears to have slid off the top of the mountain and stuck halfway down. A tiny grey church stands at the foot of the hill just above the cluster of farm buildings that is all there is of the village of Pilleth. To the left is the River Lugg, flowing swiftly among the few fields it has succeeded in taming over the millennia. And on all sides spring up the partisan hills, each one capable of sheltering a rebellious army.

No detailed description exists of the Battle of Pilleth. It may have been too confused a mêlée for an accurate account. It appears, however, to have been entirely one-sided. Young Edmund Mortimer approached Pilleth from his family land of Herefordshire. Whether he attacked the Welshmen on Bryn Glas, or whether he was ambushed, is unknown. The slaughter was considerable, though estimates range from 200 to 8,000 of Mortimer's men slain. So great was the hatred of the invaders that Welshwomen descended on the field after the battle and castrated the English corpses.

Sir Edmund met an easier fate. After a spell of captivity he married one of Owen's daughters. He remained loyal to Wales, dying seven years later during the siege of Harlech Castle.

Owen and his country failed to fulfil their imagined destiny in ten subsequent years of struggle with the English. But resisting to the last, Owen Glendower passed into history as an heroic symbol of the Welsh nation.

Beneath the steep side of Bryn Glas, a possible site of the battle, stands the isolated church of Pilleth (right).

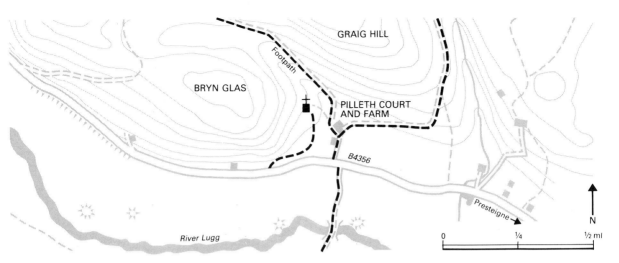

GRAIG HILL

Footpath

BRYN GLAS

PILLETH COURT
AND FARM

B4356

Presteigne →

River Lugg

N

0   ¼   ½ ml

One of the best views of the battlefield at Pilleth is from the main road. From Presteigne drive north-west along the B4356. In about five miles, just past the village of Whitton, you will see the unmistakable slope of Bryn Glas with its four central pine trees, rising to the right of the road. This was the reputed position of Owen Glendower, and this was the first view that Edmund Mortimer, approaching along the same route, had of the Welsh army.

Turn right up to the church on a gravel track 200 yards after passing Pilleth Court and Farm. It is difficult to believe that the English reached even this far in their assault, so impregnable does Bryn Glas appear from its base. It is easier to believe, as the ordnance survey apparently does, that the battle was fought on the land immediately to the south below you, along the banks of the River Lugg. A track leaving the main road opposite Pilleth Court leads across these fields to the river. (The grassy remains of an ancient fortification, marked as Castell foel-allt on the ordnance map, played no part in the battle.) Whether the Welsh army was stationed on the slopes of Bryn Glas or on these lower fields, it is likely that the subsequent slaughter spilled out across the valley as the English tried to escape.

For a splendid view of the valley and the battlefield, walk along the track leading right through the buildings of Pilleth Farm. This climbs steeply up the shoulder of Graig Hill. To the south, deep among the hills, is the narrow plain of the Lugg valley; to the west the face of Bryn Glas. For a hilly walk of about three miles with marvellous views, you can continue around Graig Hill, descending into Pilleth by the steep valley to the north of Bryn Glas. Consult O.S. map number 137 for this and many other attractive expeditions in the area.

The Battle of Homildon Hill

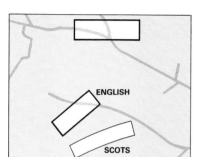

From the broad summit of Humbleton Hill in Northumberland is a wonderfully varied view. To the north is the rich plain where the Rivers Glen and Till meet on their way to join the Tweed near Berwick. Immediately to the east, pressed against the base of the hills, is the town of Wooler; beyond it the rolling land ends in a strip of ocean. The south and west give way to the Cheviots, miles of tumultuous wilderness of which Humbleton Hill is an unassuming first step.

It was called Homildon Hill in 1402 when the Scots, led by Archibald, Earl of Douglas, took up a position on its precipitous slopes. The only view they were interested in obtaining was of an English army, blocking their way back to Scotland.

Douglas had reason to be cautious but not to be alarmed. Taking advantage of Henry IV's preoccupation with Wales and the rebellious Owen Glendower, he had led his large army on a particularly successful raid into English territory. They had penetrated as far as Newcastle, leaving nothing of value that they could remove and sparing nothing valueless that they could destroy. As a result his men were tired and his army encumbered with booty, when he learned that an English army under the Percys of Northumberland had cut off his route to the north-west. Homildon Hill seemed an impregnable position for a powerful army reluctant to engage in battle.

Douglas had not reckoned on the English longbow, a weapon that the Scots had scarcely encountered. It was easy to manufacture, quick to fire and immensely powerful. Above all, it could be fired accurately at a range of 250 yards. Instead of resting securely on the heights of Homildon Hill, goad-

ing their opponents into launching a suicidal assault, the Scots discovered that they were a huge living target for the English bowmen. From the slopes of Harehope Hill, immediately to the west of the Scottish position, and from the valley between the two hills, English archers fired at will, scampering back out of range when Scottish bowmen made their furious sorties. This murderous game finally forced Douglas to lead a desperate charge down the hill. *"But the English archers falling back as the Scots advanced,"* wrote an eighteenth-century historian, *"and still making a furious and incessant discharge of arrows, which no armour was able to resist, the Scots were soon totally routed."* Another party under Sir John Swinton descended to their deaths, perhaps in the field known as Red Riggs at the foot of the hill. The rank and file of the Scottish army, so confident just hours before, now scattered across the plain to the north. Some drowned in the Tweed; many did not get so far:

Some fled, some died, some maimed there for ever,
That to Scotlande agayne came they never,

wrote John Harding, a poet/historian who served with Percy.

One Scot who survived was Archibald Douglas, nicknamed the Tyneman ("the loser"). He was wounded in five places and had lost an eye as well as a battle, but he made both a remarkable recovery and a political about-face. Just ten months later he lined up alongside his old enemy Henry Percy to face Henry IV and Prince "Hal" at the Battle of Shrewsbury.

From the north Homildon Hill, now called Humbleton Hill, dominates the landscape. For the heavily-laden Scottish army in 1402 it was a most deceptive haven.

Homildon is in Northumberland, two miles west of Wooler.

War	Anglo-Scottish Wars.
Date	14 September 1402.
Principal commanders	English: The Earl of Northumberland Sir Henry Percy (Hotspur). Scots: The Earl of Douglas.
Size of armies	English: Unknown. Scots: About 10,000.
Duration	Unknown.
Outcome	Defeat of Scots.
County	Northumberland.
Ord. Survey	1:50,000 map no. 75.
Nat. grid ref.	NT 9628.

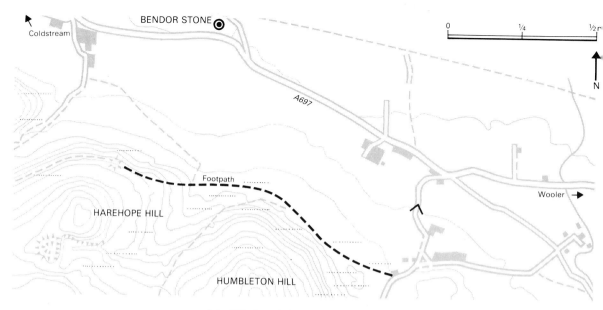

BENDOR STONE

Coldstream

A697

Footpath

Wooler →

N

0   ¼   ½

HAREHOPE HILL

HUMBLETON HILL

The morning sun climbs over Homildon Hill.

It is difficult to believe that the Scots en-camped very far up Humbleton Hill while awaiting the English. The terrain is awkward for an army laden with plunder, and even the lower slopes offer a commanding view of the plain to the north.

From Wooler drive north-west towards Coldstream along the A697. In about a mile a secondary road signposted to Humbleton Hill leads steeply to the left. In 600 yards, where the surface changes to gravel, leave your car by some picturesquely ruined buildings and follow a path that leads from the gate to the right. You are now walking north-west along the side of Humbleton Hill. Ahead is Harehope Hill, from which English longbowmen tormented the help-less Scots with volleys of arrows. To your right, in the flat fields by the road below, is the scene of the final rout of the Scots. The views to the north and north-west are breathtaking, but this path considerably follows the contours of Humbleton Hill and does not leave the energetic hiker breath-less. It is well worth the brief scramble up to the summit for even more spectacular views in all directions.

Those who can bear to descend will find that the main road to Coldstream leads through the centre of the battlefield. O.S. map no. 75 shows a right of way leading from the A697 across a field 150 yards west of the Humbleton Hill turning. This goes straight through cultivated land and may not be an attractive route during the grow-ing season, but it gives a good impression of the great wall of the Cheviots upon which the Scots believed themselves safe.

The Bendor Stone, which traditionally marks the centre of the battle, stands alone and lichen-covered on a little island of grass in a field to the north of the road, a mile to the west of the turning to Humbleton Hill.

In the fields to the north of Homildon Hill (left) occurred some of the worst slaughter, as the fleeing Scots were cut down by the Earl of Northumberland's vengeful army.

From what seemed a strong position on Homildon Hill, the Scots had a commanding view of the plain to the north (below).

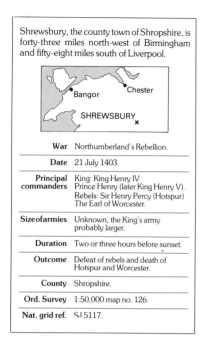

Battlefield church was built soon after the Battle of Shrewsbury. The noise of motor and rail traffic fail to penetrate the spirit of its neglected graveyard.

Shrewsbury, the county town of Shropshire, is forty-three miles north-west of Birmingham and fifty-eight miles south of Liverpool.

War	Northumberland's Rebellion.
Date	21 July 1403.
Principal commanders	King: King Henry IV Prince Henry (later King Henry V). Rebels: Sir Henry Percy (Hotspur) The Earl of Worcester.
Size of armies	Unknown, the King's army probably larger.
Duration	Two or three hours before sunset.
Outcome	Defeat of rebels and death of Hotspur and Worcester.
County	Shropshire.
Ord. Survey	1:50,000 map no. 126.
Nat. grid ref.	SJ5117.

The Battle of Shrewsbury

The fifteenth century, the cruellest hundred years in British history, got off to an appropriately bloody start. Henry IV, who had seized the throne from Richard II in 1399, immediately found himself embroiled in border wars with the elusive Welshman Owen Glendower. The northern border was no quieter. In Northumberland the Percy family was hard-pressed to resist the incursions of the Douglases from Scotland. It was to aid their efforts that Henry moved northwards in July 1403. He had got as far as the midlands when he discovered that Henry Percy (known as Hotspur), the man he was going to assist, was in open rebellion and moving south to join forces with Owen Glendower. Henry, realizing that such an alliance could put an end to his reign, assembled an army and moved with all haste towards Shrewsbury, a principal northern route into Wales, to intercept Henry Percy.

He won the race. Percy, who arrived at Shrewsbury too late to gain the safety of the west bank of the Severn, sought a place to stand and fight. The area he chose, now called Battlefield, is three miles north of Shrewsbury. A ridge running east-west offers a strong position among the flat surrounding fields. To the south the land dips and

rises again slightly before levelling off in a plain that extends to Shrewsbury. It is farmland still, though the town has stretched to within a mile of the little church built to commemorate the battle. A grim line of electricity pylons march across the fields to the south, but this unsightly intrusion, together with the distant noise of trains and traffic, only serves to isolate Battlefield Church even further from the industrial world. The church and its graveyard, the heart of this field, form an oasis of melancholy.

Hotspur deployed his men along the ridge to the north of the church. Henry, marching from Shrewsbury, was forced to draw up facing north, about a quarter mile away. There followed lengthy negotiations, but at last it was resolved that there was no alternative to battle, and the hostilities began with a murderous rain of arrows. Although they outnumbered their opponents, Henry's men fared worse in this exchange. One poetic contemporary compared the king's men scattered on the ground to "apples fallen in the autumn". The hand-to-hand combat that ensued was particularly savage. King Henry was himself forced to withdraw when Harry Hotspur and a group of followers made straight for him

through the mêlée. At least two knights volunteered to disguise themselves as the king in order to divert attention from Henry, and for their pains they both died. Some accounts attribute wonderful courage to Prince Henry, then not yet sixteen, who is thought to have commanded the left flank of his father's army. Wounded in the face by an arrow, he stayed on the field – or so claim the more fulsome historians. (Shakespeare contributed to these legends in *Henry IV, Part I*, a play in which Hotspur is made to be the same age as Prince Hal.) Hotspur was not so lucky. The arrow that struck him in the face killed him, and with that one shot the battle was effectively over. Retreat, slaughter, pilfering, burial and ruthless executions – the inevitable aftermath of any fifteenth-century battle – continued for a few days.

Hotspur was buried, but soon afterwards, in order to prove to the people that their hero was truly dead, the king had his defeated enemy exhumed, beheaded and quartered. Each quarter was warningly displayed in the four cities of Chester, Bristol, Newcastle and London, while the head was reserved for the citizens of York, who were to grow accustomed to such grisly sights during the next hundred years.

King Henry IV, victor at the Battle of Shrewsbury, strikes a belligerent posture on the east front of the church he endowed to commemorate the event.

The forlorn church at Battlefield is the starting point for any exploration of the field at Shrewsbury. Take the A49 for Whitchurch north out of Shrewsbury. In about three miles, 200 yards past the junction with the A53, turn left on a secondary road. This leads directly to the isolated church, supposed to mark the centre of the battlefield. A weathered statue of King Henry IV stands high on the east front, overlooking the gloomy churchyard.

Take the stile leading south out of the churchyard. In fifty yards turn right and follow a footpath west between fields of grain. You are in the middle of the battlefield. To your right the land slopes down and then rises to the low ridge believed to have been the position of Harry Hotspur's army. King Henry and Prince Hal occupied the flat land to your left. In about 600 yards this path becomes a track which leads to the A528, the Shrewsbury-Wrexham road.

The legend that Owen Glendower watched the battle from an oak tree is supported only by the flourishing community of mature oaks in the vicinity of the field.

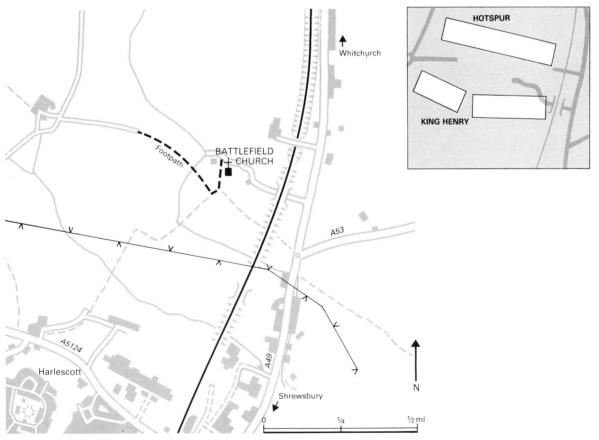

The Battle of Blore Heath

There were months, even years, during the Wars of the Roses when it appeared that greed, animosity and the lust for vengeance might finally be subsiding. Such a lull occurred during the early days of the conflict, after the first Battle of St. Albans in 1455. King Henry VI and Queen Margaret, the Lancastrian leaders, still reigned; Richard Duke of York still believed his claim to the throne was stronger. But early in 1458 the nobles of both factions assembled in London at the king's command and came to what appeared to be a joyful accord. On the twenty-fifth of March, in what must have been the most remarkable political parade London has ever seen, the king led this smiling company of dukes and earls through the streets to St. Paul's Cathedral. Two by two they marched, Yorkist and Lancastrian paired in a symbolic union. Queen Margaret took the arm of the Duke of York (whose head she later ordered impaled on the gates of York). The reconciliation did not last the year. When a brawl broke out in London between followers of the king and the Earl of Warwick, both sides prepared again for war.

The Battle of Blore Heath, the first major engagement after hostilities were renewed, did nothing except stir up fresh hatreds and reduce the male population of Cheshire by about 2,000. It was fought between the Earl of Salisbury, father of Warwick and a dedicated follower of the Duke of York, and Lord Audley, the king's representative. Audley's purpose was to stop the earl from joining the Duke of York at Ludlow in Shropshire. It is not known which army arrived at Blore Heath first, the earl advancing west or Audley marching east. As it was, both armies discovered a strong position on land that rises on either side of Hempmill Brook. The fields cut into six uneven pieces by the A53, a secondary road that crosses it,

Blore Heath is in Staffordshire, two and a half miles east of Market Drayton (Shropshire) on the A53.

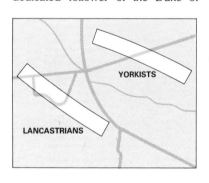

War	The Wars of the Roses.
Date	23 September 1459.
Principal commanders	Lancastrians: Lord Audley. Yorkists: The Earl of Salisbury.
Size of armies	The Lancastrians, with about 10,000 men, outnumbered the Yorkists.
Duration	Unknown.
Outcome	Defeat of the Lancastrians and death of Audley.
County	Staffordshire.
Ord. Survey	1:50,000 map no. 127.
Nat. grid ref.	SJ 7135.

and the stream that flows under their intersection and which once separated the armies. In 1459 it was partly wooded and unenclosed. Salisbury, as he paused on the eastern ridge, could see only the pennons of Audley's army above the low trees on the west of the field. Realizing that to advance would be suicidal, he drew up his army in a line extending maybe 600 yards, protecting his left flank with the stream and his right with his supply waggons. Audley must have thought twice about attacking this formidable position, but he had orders from the queen to bring back Salisbury alive or dead, and he outnumbered his opponent. Seeing the earl apparently withdrawing, Audley rushed down into the boggy valley against a cloud of arrows and struggled up the opposing slope. But Salisbury had only feigned retreat, and discovering that Audley had committed his men to an assault, he charged down the hill, catching the Lancastrians before they had completely cleared the brook.

At some point in the thick of battle Lord Audley fell. A very old cross with a worn inscription stands halfway up the Yorkist slope, presumably marking the point where he died. Salisbury had to wait another year before his head decorated the walls of York.

Like an Indian summer, the reconciliation between York and Lancaster had thus abruptly come to an end, but the Battle of Blore Heath was only the first snowfall of a very long winter.

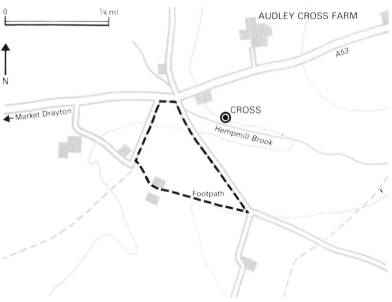

To reach Blore Heath take the A53 east out of Market Drayton towards Newcastle-under-Lyme. In just over two miles, turn right at a cross-roads on a secondary road to Hales. The actual battlefield is now to your left behind a high hedge and across the valley formed by Hempmill Brook. It is all on private land that is inaccessible to the public, but by continuing about 600 yards to the point where this road forks and taking the path across the field through the gate to your right, you get a view of the field that Lord Audley would still recognize. Walk along this path 100 yards or so, skirting a field of grain. You are now on a low ridge, the right flank of Lord Audley's position. To your right is the sloping field leading up to Lord Salisbury's ridge. His line, like Audley's, probably extended on both sides of the A53, passing very near Audley Cross Farm, which is visible on the horizon. The place on Salisbury's hill where Audley fell is marked by a cross which is totally obscured by foliage in the summer. For a circuit of this half of Audley's position, continue another

A view from the south-west (above). Hempmill Brook runs among the trees beyond the field.

The anvil now in Mucklestone churchyard is said to have been used to reshoe Queen Margaret's horse.

300 yards until a track to the right leads you back to the A53.

A curious legend concerning the Battle of Blore Heath concerns the escape of Queen Margaret, who is improbably supposed to have been watching the battle from the tower of Mucklestone church. When defeat appeared imminent she rode away with the shoes of her horse reversed to confuse pursuers. Mucklestone, a mile and a half north-east of Blore Heath, still celebrates this legend. Continue east along the A53 and turn left for Mucklestone at Ashley Heath. An ancient anvil, said to have been used for shoeing Margaret's horse, stands in the churchyard. The house opposite occupies the site of the old smithy, while in the dark church a framed description of the battle, claims, among other things, that Hempmill Brook ran red for three days after the engagement.

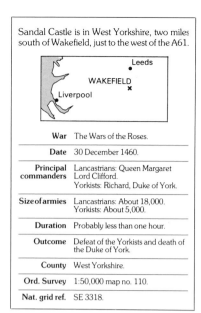

War	The Wars of the Roses.
Date	30 December 1460.
Principal commanders	Lancastrians: Queen Margaret Lord Clifford. Yorkists: Richard, Duke of York.
Size of armies	Lancastrians: About 18,000. Yorkists: About 5,000.
Duration	Probably less than one hour.
Outcome	Defeat of the Yorkists and death of the Duke of York.
County	West Yorkshire.
Ord. Survey	1:50,000 map no. 110.
Nat. grid ref.	SE 3318.

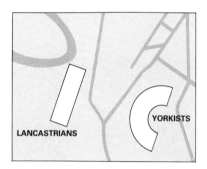

The Battle of Wakefield

Sandal Castle, on the southern outskirts of Wakefield, is a majestic ruin, its walls long worn down by violence and neglect. In December 1460 it was a powerful fortress, forbidding enough to provide protection for Richard Duke of York from a huge Lancastrian army. The city of Wakefield has since advanced untidily towards its walls, but the castle is still an eloquent relic of the Wars of the Roses.

In early December 1460, Richard had nearly achieved his ambitions. Although he had failed to depose Henry VI and declare himself Richard III, he had extracted a promise from the king (his captive) and parliament that eventually his children should rule England. Queen Margaret, headstrong and free in the north of England, would have none of this agreement. Raising a powerful army, she so alarmed Richard with her growing support and righteous anger that he set out to confront her. Four days before Christmas

he arrived with 5,000 men at Sandal Castle. The Lancastrian army, at least three times as large, assembled nearby in a loose but effective siege.

Richard was an impatient man. He knew that his eldest son Edward was in Shrewsbury and would hasten to relieve him as soon as he had gathered an army, but he longed for a quick and decisive triumph over his persistent adversaries. On the thirtieth of December he rode out of his stronghold down to the unenclosed fields south of the River Calder, an area then known as Wakefield Green. Whether he was aware of the full strength of the Lancastrian army under Lord Clifford is uncertain. Some historians have suggested that he was lured out of his retreat by a small force and then crushed by a massive ambush on both flanks. Whatever happened, he was dead within an hour. His head was adorned with a paper crown and impaled on the walls of York, to "over-

look the town". In that grim vigil he was joined by many of his nobles, including his second son Edmund who, although he begged on his knees for mercy, had been stabbed in the heart by Lord Clifford after the battle. (Clifford was killed in battle three months later.)

Today Sandal Castle provides a splendid view, but not one that is of much help to the visitor trying to recreate the Battle of Wakefield. Farmland to the south-west is pleasantly rural, but Wakefield Green is green no longer. Modern brick houses slice into the fields to the north-west and the south. Cooling towers and industry unsettle the mind in search of a medieval scene. The plain to the west is scarred by construction and flooded with great amoeba-shaped ponds. The whole landscape is a visual history of industrial Britain. In the midst of it all Sandal Castle stands aloof. Though roofless and crumbling, it still offers sanctuary from the siege without.

Sandal Castle overlooks the plain immediately south of Wakefield. In December 1460 it was besieged by a vast Lancastrian army under Queen Margaret and her general, Lord Clifford. Inside was Richard, Duke of York, whose claim to the throne had aroused the queen's hatred. Though quite secure within his stronghold, Richard incredibly chose to attack, a venture which cost him his life.

Only grassy mounds and a few ragged walls remain of the castle that protected Richard of York.

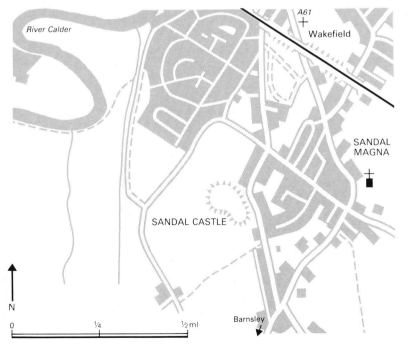

The Battle of Wakefield was fought on the flat land to the north and west of Sandal Castle. These fields are neither easy nor rewarding to visit, but the castle itself is a splendid ruin and provides views of Wakefield and the surrounding countryside. To reach the castle leave Wakefield on the A61 towards Barnsley. After passing Sandal Magna church (about two miles) turn right on Castle Road and left at the cross-roads. The castle is on a hill straight ahead, its walls and keep overlooking the partly-flooded plain to the west, a scene of much of the fighting.

The A61 crosses the river Calder over a new bridge. The little chapel long believed to have been built by Edward IV to commemorate the brutal murder of his brother Edmund is on the old bridge to the left as you leave Wakefield. The visible structure is Victorian Gothic.

Wakefield Museum (open Monday to Saturday 12:30-5:30; Sunday 2:30-5:30) has an excellent model of Sandal Castle as it appeared in the fifteenth century.

55

The Battle of Mortimer's Cross

"Dazzle mine eyes, or do I see three suns?" asked Edward Duke of York (according to Shakespeare) on the morning of the second of February 1461. What he actually saw was a parhelion or mock sun, an illusion created by the refraction of light through ice crystals, but if he knew this he did not admit it. To his soldiers, waiting at Mortimer's Cross for a Lancastrian army advancing from Wales, he claimed this phenomenon was a sure sign of victory, and the entire army knelt down in prayer.

Less than a month had passed since Edward had learned of his father's death at the Battle of Wakefield. The shock of this news, however, only strengthened his resolve to raise a powerful army on the Welsh border. He realized that he was the one man who could rally the Yorkist cause, and as such was sure to be the principal object of any future Lancastrian campaign. And Edward was not loth to encounter Queen Margaret. His father's head was still skewered high on the walls of York, a perpetual encitement to revenge.

He did not have long to wait. As he marched east to intercept Margaret on her way to London, Edward learned that a small Lancastrian force, led by the Earls of Pembroke and Wiltshire, was pursuing him. At Mortimer's Cross he wheeled around to face west and meet his enemy. The parhelion was a godsend, exactly the sort of fillip he needed to inspire his men.

The place where Edward made his stand has changed little in 500 years (though the Mortimer's Cross Garage might surprise him even more than the apparition of three suns). A stone cross may once have marked the spot, but two roads form the only cross today, one travelling north-south, the other roughly east-west. Edward defended this latter route. It crosses the River Lugg to the east and climbs the low hill towards Croft Castle. To the west is the mountainous interior of Wales, a daunting land for any Englishman to face in battle. It is here, at Mortimer's Cross, that the Lugg slows down on its race from the hills, meandering towards Kingsland over rich pastureland.

At first sight this is not a very promising position. The river offered Edward a hazardous retreat, but he evidently intended that the Lancastrians should be allowed no means of avoiding battle, as they would if he had chosen to face them from across the river. The combat was extremely one-sided. Some accounts suggest that the Lancastrians prevailed on their left wing, but in the centre Edward soon had his opponents retreating towards Kingsland, their corpses scattered over the marshy meadows that lie between the river and the road.

Nearly 4,000 Lancastrians died that day. The Earls of Pembroke and Wiltshire managed to escape, but not so Pembroke's father. Old Sir Owen Tudor was captured and taken to Hereford, where he was beheaded. It is said that he did not believe he was actually going to die until his doublet was torn from his shoulders as he stood before the block. The head was stuck upon the market cross. Edward's revenge on Queen Margaret had begun.

Mortimer's Cross is a village in Hereford and Worcester on the A4110, seventeen miles north of Hereford.	
War	The Wars of the Roses.
Date	2 February 1461.
Principal commanders	Lancastrians: The Earls of Pembroke and Wiltshire. Yorkists: Edward Duke of York (later King Edward IV).
Size of armies	Unknown, the Yorkists outnumbering the Lancastrians.
Duration	Unknown.
Outcome	Defeat of the Lancastrians.
County	Hereford and Worcester.
Ord. Survey	1:50,000 map no. 137.
Nat. grid ref.	SO 4263.

The fields immediately south of Mortimer's Cross were the scene of some of the heaviest fighting. The Yorkists fought with their backs to the River Lugg.

A stone bridge crosses the River Lugg at the point where Edward made his stand against the advancing Lancastrians under Jasper Tudor.

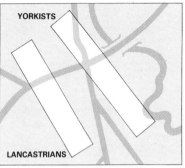

Mortimer's Cross is little more now than it was in 1461 – a cross-roads, an inn and a few houses. Only the traffic and the Mortimer's Cross Garage would puzzle Prince Edward today. He drew up here between the road that is now the A4110 and the River Lugg, facing west in order to confront the Earl of Pembroke's army. The land immediately to the north of the bridge, where the Lancastrians launched their first successful attack, is not accessible, but the meadows to the south can be reached through a gate just fifty feet west of the river. It was here, where the river meanders through flat pastures, that Edward broke the Lancastrian army, chasing them south towards Kingsland.

At Kingsland is the battle monument, or pedestal as it calls itself. It stands in front of The Monument public house, on the corner of the A4110 and the B4360, and is unusually informative, though its claim that this battle established Edward as king is stretching the truth a bit. The Battle of Towton was a more conclusive affair.

Croft Castle, two miles east of Mortimer's Cross off the B4362, is a magnificently maintained building and is well worth a visit. In 1461 it was the home of Sir Richard Croft, a valuable ally of Edward.

It is open May to end of September, Wednesday to Sunday (including Bank Holiday Mondays) 2-6; April and October, Saturday and Sunday (including Easter Monday) 2-6.

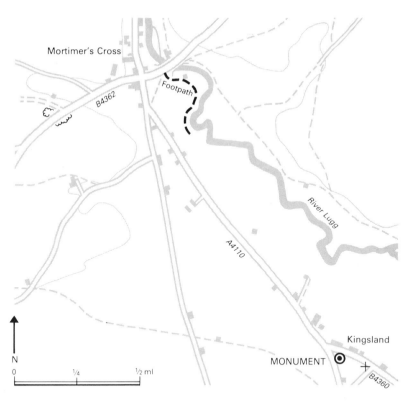

Thickets and undergrowth to the south of the bridge make exploring parts of the field at Mortimer's Cross a battle in itself. Much of the land, however, is clear.

Croft Castle (right), formidable residence of Edward's ally Sir Richard Croft, was only two miles behind the Yorkist line, offering a secure haven in defeat.

The Battle of Towton

Towton was the bloodiest battle ever fought on British soil. Estimates vary as to the number of dead, but 28,000 is the lowest given in any early account. The shallow valley between the two ridges where the armies stood was thick with corpses, and the little Cock Beck was such an obstacle to the retreating Lancastrians *"that men alive passed the river upon dead carcasses"*. Prior to the battle the nineteen year-old Edward IV gave orders that no prisoners should be taken; afterwards he paid his gravediggers extra for their herculean task. They must have thanked God for unseasonably cold weather that kept the stench at bay.

It is hard to imagine what spasm of loyalty, fear or hatred could have sent two per cent of the total population of England into a field, to kill each other in hand-to-hand combat. Only the political facts of the event are understandable today. After the defeat of Richard Duke of York at Wakefield, his son

Edward raised an army in the west and surprised his Lancastrian enemies by entering London and proclaiming himself king. No sooner had he done so that he set out for the north in pursuit of the woman who still called herself Queen Margaret and whose husband was King Henry VI. It may have occurred to him that this was precisely what his father had done just three months earlier, an expedition that ended in his death, but Edward was a young man with a lust for battle.

The queen, her enormous army commanded by the twenty-four year-old Duke of Somerset, awaited him near Towton in Yorkshire. There were preliminary skirmishes at Ferrybridge, where the Lancastrians prevailed, and another at Dintingdale, very near Towton, where the tables were turned and Lord Clifford "the butcher" died with a headless arrow in his throat. Then, on the twenty-eighth of March, Edward assembled his men in a line a

mile long on a ridge half a mile to the south of the Lancastrian army.

The next day was Palm Sunday, but only Henry VI asked for the impending slaughter to be postponed. For Edward the conditions were favourable. He had a strong wind at his back, and soon after nine o'clock it began to snow. His archers advanced several paces and each shot one arrow. Without advancing, the Lancastrians shot back recklessly into the storm. Their arrows fell short, and the Yorkists returned the volley to deadly effect. Provoked into action, the Lancastrians advanced down the hill and up against Edward's army. Of the mayhem that ensued no one has left any clear description, except that it lasted for ten hours. In the crush of soldiers many fell from exhaustion, to be trampled to death by their own replacements. Somewhere during the day Edward may have received reinforcements from the Duke of Norfolk. By evening his army was

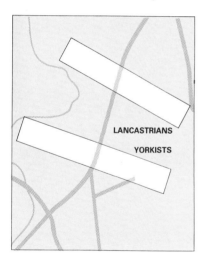

A view from the south of the battlefield. The dark ridge in the distance is that on which King Edward's men assembled to face Somerset's massive army.

Lord Dacre's weathered cross stands by the side of the B1217, on the northern half of the battlefield. This was the ridge held by the Lancastrians. They faced south and had the misfortune of attacking into the teeth of a fierce late-winter snow storm. Lord Dacre, a local nobleman, was one of their thousands of casualties.

slowly gaining ground. When the Lancastrians finally broke ranks and retreated, the real butchery began.

The road that runs from Towton to Saxton did not exist in 1461. An unenclosed and trackless moor stretched between the two armies. Today the field has a domestic appearance. It is hard to imagine that it could contain so many bodies, dead or alive. From Lord Dacre's memorial on the Lancastrian ridge the land dips gently before climbing to the Yorkist position. It is only from the road in the valley below that one sees the steepening sides of the slopes as the land falls away to Cock Beck. In this little gully thousands of soldiers lay dead at the end of the day. *"The soil is remarkable,"* says a nineteenth-century author, *"for producing rich rank grass."*

The day after the battle Edward entered York and removed his father's head from the city wall. He replaced it with fresh trophies of his own.

Towton is a village in North Yorkshire, three miles south of Tadcaster on the A162.

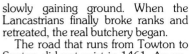

War	The Wars of the Roses.
Date	29 March 1461.
Principal commanders	Lancastrians: The Duke of Somerset. Yorkists: King Edward IV.
Size of armies	Both armies were enormous, each probably numbering more than 30,000. The Lancastrians slightly outnumbered the Yorkists.
Duration	Ten hours, from morning until dark.
Outcome	Victory for the Yorkists. Total dead: 20-30,000.
County	North Yorkshire.
Ord. Survey	1:50,000 map no. 105.
Nat. grid ref.	SE 4738.

The easiest way to identify the battlefield at Towton is to find the cross erected as a memorial to Lord Dacre, a Lancastrian nobleman who was killed in the battle. From the village of Towton take the B1217 south-west to Garforth. The cross, a weathered stone column, is on the right of the road in three-quarters of a mile. You are now standing on a low ridge, the right flank of the Lancastrian position. Clearly visible ahead to the south is the ridge where the Yorkist army prepared for battle. Between these two heights is the depression where much of the fighting took place. Continue slowly along the road. The land to your right at the bottom of Towton Dale falls away steeply. Bloody Meadow and the Cock Beck are just out of sight, but this entire area was piled with the dead and dying by the end of the day.

At the top of the ridge look back to the cross and the Lancastrian position from a Yorkist point of view. The highest land on the field (167 ft.) is immediately to your right. Neither army had an obvious positional advantage.

A pleasant walk (though muddy in winter) of about a mile from Towton Village along the Old London Road takes you to a small wooden bridge over the Cock Beck. Now a delightful wooded valley, in 1461 this was a horrific morass of mud and Lancastrian corpses.

In Saxton churchyard, on the north side, is the modest tomb where both Lord Dacre and his horse lie buried.

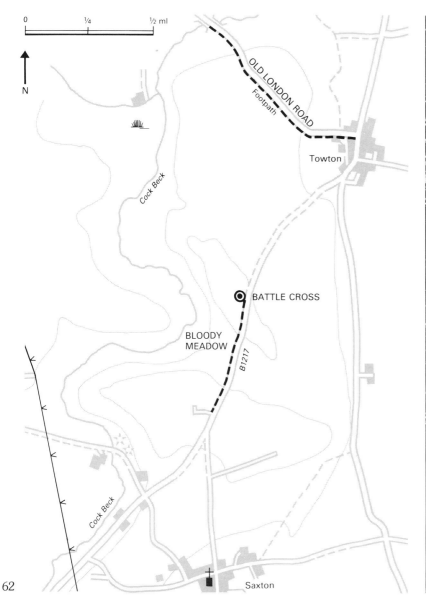

Lord Dacre's unassuming tomb in Saxton churchyard is invested with an unseen interest: both the man and his horse lie beneath the stone. He was a Lancastrian casualty.

The Old London Road from the village of Towton crosses the Cock Beck on this bridge. In 1461 the river near here was deep with the Lancastrian dead (below).

The Battle of Edgcote

Of all the ways to lose a battle, the Earls of Pembroke and Devon contrived to find the most absurd at Edgcote.

After four years of relative peace, the Yorkist kingdom of Edward IV was again under threat from the Lancastrians and their supporters. In Kent an army under the Earl of Warwick, formerly the king's greatest ally, advanced on London, while in Yorkshire Sir John Conyers marched south with a large band of discontented rebels. To counter this latter threat, Edward ordered the Earls of Pembroke and Devon to intercept Conyers and his northerners. The two armies met, almost by accident, near Edgcote, a village six miles north-east of Banbury.

The battle was fought on the twenty-sixth of July; it was lost on the evening of the twenty-fourth, when the Earl of Pembroke, using his seniority, ousted his brother-in-arms Devon from a Banbury inn (possibly *the* inn). This broke a first-come-first-serve agree-ment the two officers had made regarding accommodation, but Devon was particularly annoyed because he was infatuated with one of the ladies of the house. Denied both his bed and his bawd, he stormed out of town, taking with him his powerful band of archers.

Pembroke returned to a depleted army on Edgcote Hill. He was heartened by victory in a skirmish on the evening of the twenty-fifth, but the next morning the northerners came down in force from their hill position and attacked the Yorkists with arrows. Unable to return their shot without Devon's archers, the Lancastrians descended and met their opponents on Danes Moor. In savage hand-to-hand combat Pembroke and his brother (who twice rode through the enemy line wielding a poleax *"and without any mortall wounde returned"*) fought bravely, but they were at length captured. Both were taken to Banbury and beheaded. On Danes Moor, nearly 4,000 of their followers had undergone a less ceremonious fate. As for the Earl of Devon, he fled to Somerset where, according to Hall's *Chronicle "he was taken and brought to Bridgwater, and there cut shorter by the hedde"*.

Danes Moor is a broad valley traversed by a stream. Early accounts mention three surrounding hills; there are in fact more. It is not an easy field from which to escape. The River Cherwell forms its northern boundary and closes the trap. In the panic of retreat a lucky few of Pembroke's men stumbled across the water to safety. It is farmland now, though there is still rough ground down by the stream. To the west rises Edgcote Hill surmounted by Edgcote Lodge, its forbidding walls as appropriate to a fortress as to a farm. No such walls sheltered Pembroke's archerless army in 1469. And all for the sake of a room in the inn and a barmaid in Banbury.

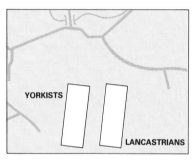

YORKISTS

LANCASTRIANS

Edgcote is a tiny Northamptonshire village, six miles north-east of Banbury (Oxfordshire).

× EDGCOTE

• Oxford

London •

War	The Wars of the Roses.
Date	26 July 1469.
Principal commanders	Lancastrians: Sir John Conyers. Yorkists: The Earl of Pembroke.
Size of armies	Unknown, the Lancastrians considerably outnumbering the Yorkists.
Duration	Unknown.
Outcome	Defeat of the Yorkists. Capture and execution of Pembroke.
County	Northamptonshire.
Ord. Survey	1:50,000 maps nos. 151 and 152.
Nat. grid ref.	SP 5146.

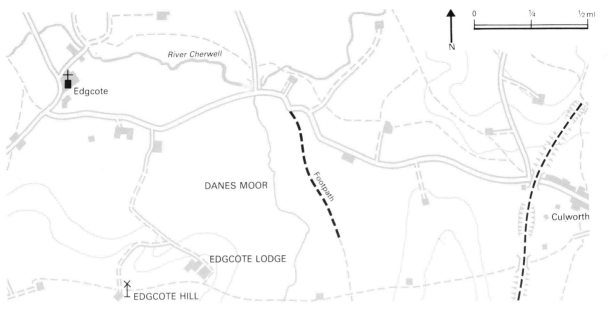

A circle of brick frames a field near Culworth, an area held by the Lancastrians prior to the Battle of Edgcote.

Contemporary accounts of the Battle of Edgcote refer to three hills, but their exact location is uncertain. Blackbird Hill, to the north-east of Danes Moor, may have been one of the Lancastrian positions on the eve of the battle.

The best place to start an exploration of the battlefield at Edgcote is on Danes Moor, the low land immediately to the west of Culworth. From Banbury take the A361 towards Daventry. In five miles turn right for Edgcote at the village of Wardington. At Edgcote drive towards Culworth, stopping in just over a mile, where the road bends sharp left. A track on the right leads straight across Danes Moor, where most of the fighting took place. Ahead to your right is Edgcote Hill, where Pembroke's men encamped the night before the battle. They were forced down to Danes Moor and hand-to-hand combat when unable to repel the might of the Lancastrian archers. The Lancastrians occupied the high land straight ahead to the south of Danes Moor, descending to challenge the Yorkists on the morning of the twenty-sixth of July.

A third hill, one to the east, plays a crucial part in the battle. It was over this hill that a mere 500 Lancastrian reinforcements charged down on the field. Fearing that the entire army of the Earl of Warwick had arrived, the Yorkists lost heart and fled. Many would have attempted to cross the little River Cherwell, which flows among the fields to the north of Danes Moor.

For an excellent panoramic view of the battlefield, return towards Edgcote, turning left in about half a mile at the drive marked Trafford Bridge Farm and Edgcote Lodge. This leads up Edgcote Hill, the Yorkist position, from which Danes Moor and the surrounding hills are clearly visible.

Edgcote church has been unaffected by the events of 1469 but is worth visiting for its marvellous Elizabethan monuments.

The Battle of Tewkesbury

On the floor of the choir in Tewkesbury Abbey is a small diamond of polished brass. *"Hic jacet Eduardus . . .,"* reads the inscription, *"Here lies Edward Prince of Wales, cruelly slain while but a youth, Anno Domini 1471 May fourth. Alas the savagery of men. Thou art the sole light of thy mother, the last hope of thy race."* This is a humble monument to an event that nearly ended the Wars of the Roses. The death of Edward, only son of Henry VI and Queen Margaret, so dispirited the Lancastrian faction that Edward IV of York reigned for twelve years of relative peace. (He died in 1483 of over-indulgence, a natural death for one of his temperament, and England plunged once more into civil war.)

Such a vision of the future did not appear to Kind Edward at Tredington on the evening of the third of May. His army was outnumbered by Queen Margaret's, camped just three miles away at Tewkesbury. His men were exhausted, having marched nearly thirty miles that day in order to catch the Lancastrians before they crossed the River Severn. But if she once gained the freedom of Wales and the north, Edward knew, Margaret could raise an army that would make her present force look like a detachment of pickets. Since hearing of her arrival at Weymouth twenty days previously, Edward had realized the necessity of forcing an early encounter.

Queen Margaret, for her part, was not fighting the battle of her choice. On the fourteenth of April, the very day she landed in England, her ally the Earl of Warwick died at the Battle of Barnet, his army routed by the Yorkists under the command of Edward. When she heard this news, Margaret's first inclination was to return immediately to France, but she was persuaded to join forces with her friends in the north. During the next three weeks, recruiting in the south-west so delayed her that she could not escape a confrontation with Edward. At Tewkesbury, making the best of a bad situation, she ensured that her army was in a strong position, left it under the command of the Duke of Somerset, and withdrew a womanly distance from the field of battle.

On the morning of the fourth of May Somerset and his army faced south, their backs to the abbey, each flank protected by a little brook. In front of him the land fell away slightly, *"afore them and upon every hand of them, foul lanes and deep dikes and many hedges, with hills and valleys, a right evil place to approach".* Somerset himself took the right flank; young Prince Edward shared command of the centre with Lord Wenlock; the Earl of Devonshire held the left flank. Facing them, 600 yards to the south stood the army of Kind Edward, only partially visible across this unwelcoming field.

The action that followed was as confused as the terrain itself. Worsted in an exchange of cannon fire and arrows, Somerset advanced in an attempt to outflank his opponents. He encountered instead the left centre of the Yorkist line, and found himself out-flanked by King Edward's brother Richard (later Richard III) and 200 spearmen who had been concealed in nearby woods. To add to his discomfiture, Somerset received no support from his own centre and left flank. After a grim hand-to-hand struggle, his men were forced back. Retreat turned to panic. In the confused alarm of rumour and fear, the Lancastrian army fled for their lives. Hundreds were slaughtered in attempting to reach the safety of the Severn. Others died in the abbey grounds, while the abbey itself provided no sanctuary. According to one account, Somerset split open the head of Lord Wenlock, his own general. And somewhere in this mêlée Prince Edward, the pride of the House of Lancaster, fell dead.

Tewkesbury today is still a small town. When approached from the south it is the square, tower-heavy abbey that confronts the visitor, as it once rose to face King Edward. Modern houses occupy the centre of the Lancastrian line. A pyramid of red brick council offices rise beside Bloody Meadow, the strip of coarse pasture-land where so much of the slaughter occurred. But these modern incursions cannot entirely dispel a sense of antiquity. Perhaps it is the abbey that establishes this mood. It retains the detachment of ancient stone and stands aloof now as once it stood when the body of Prince Edward *"was homely interred with the other simple corpses in the church of the monastery of black monks in Tewkesbury".*

The entire battlefield can be seen through the trees on Tewkesbury Park (above). The abbey tower is just visible to the left. The Yorkists advanced from the right.

Queen Margaret is thought to have crossed the Severn at Lower Lode (below). Hundreds of her soldiers drowned or were slaughtered at the river bank.

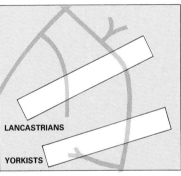

LANCASTRIANS

YORKISTS

Tewkesbury is in Gloucestershire on the A38, ten miles north of Gloucester.

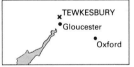

War	The Wars of the Roses.
Date	4 May 1471.
Principal commanders	Lancastrians: Queen Margaret The Duke of Somerset. Yorkists: King Edward IV.
Size of armies	Lancastrians: About 6,000. Yorkists: About 5,000.
Duration	Unknown.
Outcome	Complete defeat of the Lancastrians. Capture and imprisonment of Queen Margaret. Death of her son Prince Edward and of the Duke of Somerset.
County	Gloucestershire.
Ord. Survey	1:50,000 map no. 150.
Nat. grid ref.	SO 8931.

Modern roads and houses have eaten into much of the field at Tewkesbury, but it is still an attractive place to visit and the abbey, the dominating landmark of the town then as now, is an ideal place to begin a tour. It was in the abbey that a number of Lancastrian nobles sought sanctuary after the battle, though whether they were successful in saving their skins is a point on which contemporary historians differ. The roof of the sanctuary (above the altar) is decorated with triumphal Yorkist suns. Below is a solitary brass plaque that marks the tomb of Edward of Lancaster, only son of Henry VI, who was killed in the battle. While in the abbey, it is well worth asking to see the inside of the sacristy door. This is literally armour-plated with armour from fallen soldiers. Thick as is the steel, it is perforated with both arrow and gunshot holes.

The Vineyards, a rather bare public park to the south of the abbey, can be reached from the east of the abbey grounds by a bridge over the little River Swilgate. Here, on a hill, is an uninspiring and neglected monument to the battle.

Leaving the town by the A38 towards Gloucester, turn right opposite the hospital, immediately after crossing the Swilgate. This leads to Lower Lode, the ford that Queen Margaret is believed to have used as her escape route. Many of her soldiers met their ends here along the steep banks of the Severn in their disorderly retreat. A peace-

The inside of the sacristy door in Tewkesbury Abbey is plated with armour stripped from corpses. The hole above the horizontal bar was made by an arrow.

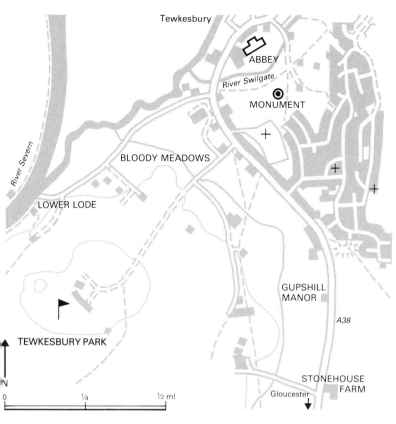

Tewkesbury

ABBEY

River Swilgate

● MONUMENT

BLOODY MEADOWS

River Severn

LOWER LODE

A38

GUPSHILL
MANOR

TEWKESBURY PARK

N

0   ¼   ½ ml

STONEHOUSE
FARM

Gloucester

ful boathouse belonging to Cheltenham College now makes the panic of 1471 seem quite improbable.

Back on the A38, continue south for another 300 yards, then turn right up to Tewkesbury Park. In 100 yards on your right you will see a sign indicating the Bloody Meadow, where hundreds of retreating Lancastrians were cut down by Edward's army.

Tewkesbury Park is a hill due east of the battlefield. It is now a golf course, but the car park provides an excellent view of the surrounding countryside. It was from this hill, then a thick wood, that 200 of Edward's spearmen launched an ambush on the Lancastrian's right flank.

Return to the main road and continue along towards Gloucester for about half a mile. Gupshill Manor (restored in 1707), the striking black and white building on your right, was in the hollow between the Lancastrian and Yorkist lines and saw much of the action 500 years ago. Today it is a pub. Just inside the entrance to the bars is a colourful plan of the battle.

Finally, at the entrance to Stonehouse Farm, 500 yards farther out of Tewkesbury on the A38, stop and look back at the abbey and the Lancastrian position as Edward would have seen it.

The museum on Barton Street (open daily 10-1 and 2-5, April to October) has a room devoted to the battle and the abbey.

The silence of Tewkesbury Abbey (left) was once shattered by the noise of battle and, according to some accounts, by the screams of Lancastrians who were murdered within its walls. A simple brass plaque marks the grave of Prince Edward.

From near Stonehouse Farm, due south of the city, one gets a Yorkist's impression of the battlefield. In 1471 the land was criss-crossed with "foul lanes and deep dikes" but then, as now, the abbey tower appeared on the horizon.

	Bosworth Field is in Leicestershire, two and a half miles south of Market Bosworth. It is well sign-posted from the main roads.

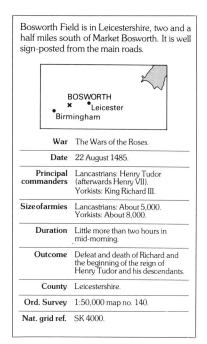

War	The Wars of the Roses.
Date	22 August 1485.
Principal commanders	Lancastrians: Henry Tudor (afterwards Henry VII). Yorkists: King Richard III.
Size of armies	Lancastrians: About 5,000. Yorkists: About 8,000.
Duration	Little more than two hours in mid-morning.
Outcome	Defeat and death of Richard and the beginning of the reign of Henry Tudor and his descendants.
County	Leicestershire.
Ord. Survey	1:50,000 map no. 140.
Nat. grid ref.	SK 4000.

The Battle of Bosworth

Bosworth is one of those rarities among English battlefields – a tourist attraction. The site has been carefully organized to provide education, relaxation and exercise, for the student, the family dog or the coach loads of school children who swarm like King Richard's soldiers over the crest of Ambion Hill.

There is good reason for the eminence of this field. Only twice have English kings died in battle in their own land. Harold, who fell at Hastings, has become a martyred hero to the sentimental readers of history. Richard III, whose naked body hung for two days on public display after the Battle of Bosworth, is still either the popular villain of English history – the king we love to hate – or a much maligned hero. His death marked the beginning of the great Tudor dynasty and the virtual end of a long and bloody civil war. But despite the confident panels that inform a visitor on his tour around the field, despite the monument marking the place of Richard's death, Bosworth is one of the more mysterious of British battlefields. No one is quite sure as to the extent of that strategic swamp, precisely where the Stanley brothers "sat on the fence" with their uncommitted armies or exactly how the king met his violent end.

An outline of the battle and of the events immediately preceding it are not in dispute. In 1485 young Henry Tudor, an exile in France, felt that he had enough support in England to risk an invasion. His claim to the throne was no greater than that of the reigning king, Richard III, but the enmity between the houses of Lancaster (Henry) and York (Richard) had not subsided. In the Wars of the Roses, while there were embers, there was still a good chance of flames.

On August the first, Henry landed at Milford Haven with 2,000 men. Three weeks later, with an added 3,000 soldiers and vague promises of more support, he faced Richard near the town of Market Bosworth in Leicestershire. Richard outnumbered his rival and was quick to seize a favourable position atop Ambion Hill, but he had

justifiable fears that his soldiers would not prove loyal. The Earl of Northumberland at the rear of his army was particularly unenthusiastic in his support. (In assembling an army Richard had encouraged his nobles to join him on pain of death.) Far more of a problem were Lord Stanley and his brother, Sir William Stanley, who arrived at the scene uncommitted to fight for either side. Henry, who had been negotiating with the Stanleys just before the battle, was as desperate as Richard for their aid. But the fighting began with the Stanleys as bystanders. Richard's troops, led by the faithful Duke of Norfolk, streamed down upon the tightly grouped formation of the Earl of Oxford. A brief exchange of arrows was followed by vicious and exhausting hand-to-hand combat with halberds, daggers, spears and swords. When neither side prevailed, Henry galloped off with a small party to seek the aid of Sir William Stanley. Richard, alarmed at this sortie, charged furiously down the hill himself and fell upon Henry's men. It was then that Sir

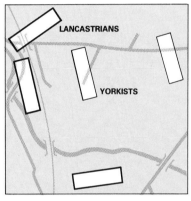

LANCASTRIANS

YORKISTS

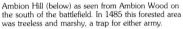

In Ambion Hill (above) King Richard had a positional advantage over the Lancastrians, but the low morale of his army and the reluctance of allies were his downfall.

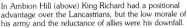

Ambion Hill (below) as seen from Ambion Wood on the south of the battlefield. In 1485 this forested area was treeless and marshy, a trap for either army.

William Stanley finally made a move. He attacked the king, who died in a savage mêlée, shouting *"Treason, treason."* That, at least, is the battlefield centre's version of his death, and it remains an attractive possibility.

Henry became Henry VII on the field and wore the crown that had fallen from Richard's head.

Bosworth Field is a festive place today. Richard's banner flutters from Ambion Hill. The book shop does a brisk trade; the model room, the film theatre and the Bosworth Buttery are attractive alternatives to a rainy walk. There are five car parks and picnic areas and four footpaths.

The field itself is set in pleasant farmland. To the south are the Ambion Woods, once clear and marshy ground, which forced Henry to move his army around to the west side of Ambion Hill. To the north is the rolling country where Sir William Stanley quietly waited, visible all the time to the infuriated king on the hill.

"What can we do at Bosworth Field?" asks the free brochure.

"You can have an unusual and exciting day out," it answers itself.

Ruefully Richard might have agreed. 71

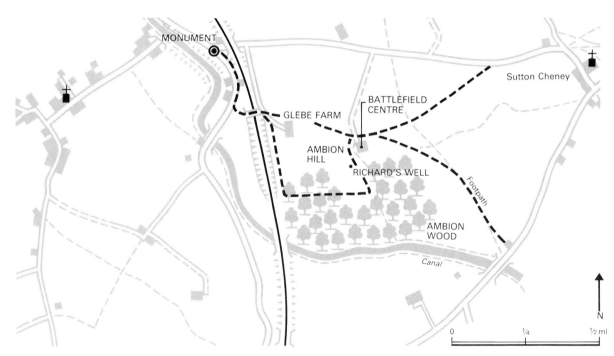

The battlefield at Bosworth is well sign-posted from the A444, the A447, the A5 and the B585, the nearest villages being Sutton Cheney, Market Bosworth and Shenton. The most convenient spot for starting a visit is the Battlefield Centre on Ambion Hill, the entrance to which is on the road from Sutton Cheney to Shenton. The centre is open 15 April to 25 October, Monday to Saturday 2-5:30; Sundays and Bank Holiday Mondays and Tuesdays (also Good Friday) 1-6. Spending a few pence on a map is a good investment, but otherwise information panels at important points along the route lead you in an anti-clockwise tour of the field.

From the car park, the path takes you behind the main scene of the fighting and provides a splendid view of the fields to the north, where Sir William Stanley hesitated on the brink of the battle. It then turns left down the hill to Shenton Station, now an information point. (A diversion here takes you to the little field with the monument claiming to be the spot where Richard died.) Continuing southwards along the circuit, you follow the main line of Henry Tudor's army. Up the hill to the left is Glebe Farm, scene of the heaviest fighting. It was down this slope that Richard's soldiers charged. Upon reaching Ambion Woods (in 1485 a discouraging swamp) turn left. Some historians believe that Lord Stanley was stationed on this side of the field, thus catching Richard in a pincer movement when his brother advanced from the north. At the end of the woods is Richard's Well (really a spring) at which the king is reputed to have drunk before the battle.

Descriptive panels guide the visitor around Bosworth Field. Glebe Farm, in the distance, stands where much of the heaviest fighting occurred.

Richard's battle standard (opposite) flutters from Ambion Hill. The whole battlefield, which has been developed as a tourist attraction, has a festive air.

In a field to the north-west of Ambion Hill is a stone marking the spot where Richard is reputed to have died crying "Treason! Treason!"

73

The Battle of Stoke

The little village of East Stoke in Nottinghamshire was the scene of one of the bloodiest and least remembered battles in British history. On the flat fields by the River Trent the desperate rebels who fought for Lambert Simnel died in their thousands as they fled the vengeance of Henry VII.

Lambert Simnel was not yet twelve years old in 1487, yet he was the symbolic leader of a group of rebels led by the Earl of Lincoln, who fraudulently claimed that the boy was King Edward VI. Lincoln and several thousand followers, including 2,000 German mercenaries, set sail from Dublin with their boy-king in tow, and landed in Lancashire on the fourth of June 1487.

The king, in Kenilworth when he heard of the invasion, assembled an army under the Earl of Oxford and marched north to confront the rebels. His soldiers' conduct on the march was governed by a formidable proclamation issued by Henry himself. This forbade them a number of soldierly pursuits, from stealing vegetables to making disturbances at night, and insisted that *"ne persones whatsoever they be, ravish no religios woman"*. Henry was not neglectful of his own duty. On Saturday the sixteenth of June he arose early and heard two masses. Then, knowing the enemy to be near, he prepared his men for battle and marched north towards Newark along the old Foss Way (now the A46).

There are few authentic descriptions

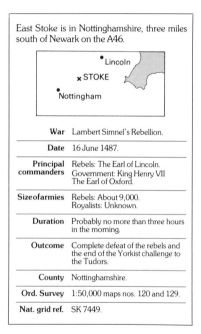

East Stoke is in Nottinghamshire, three miles south of Newark on the A46.

War	Lambert Simnel's Rebellion.
Date	16 June 1487.
Principal commanders	Rebels: The Earl of Lincoln. Government: King Henry VII The Earl of Oxford.
Size of armies	Rebels: About 9,000. Royalists: Unknown.
Duration	Probably no more than three hours in the morning.
Outcome	Complete defeat of the rebels and the end of the Yorkist challenge to the Tudors.
County	Nottinghamshire.
Ord. Survey	1:50,000 maps nos. 120 and 129.
Nat. grid ref.	SK 7449.

From the Foss Way (the modern A46) at the village of East Stoke, the land rises gradually to the long hilltop held in 1487 by the Earl of Lincoln's army.

REBELS

GOVERNMENT

The River Trent at Fiskerton (right) once provided a slender last hope for hundreds of Lincoln's retreating soldiers. Many drowned while trying to cross.

remaining of the battle. The rebels had drawn up on the hill above East Stoke and at first, confronting only the Earl of Oxford's men who led the king's army, they held their own. But as the rest of the long column arrived from the south, Henry sent the whole of his forces into battle and *"by the helpe of Almighty God,"* wrote one of his heralds, *"he had the victorye."* The victory was not a pretty one. The shabby, undisciplined Irish soldiers broke and ran for a ford over the Trent, but many were butchered in a ravine since called Red Gutter; others were hacked to death in the water meadows before they could reach safety. In all about 4,000 rebels and 3,000 of the king's men died that morning.

The scene of this final bloody pursuit is today the pleasantest part of the battlefield at Stoke. The meadows are rich agricultural land; the river is a source of recreation for patient members of the Nottingham Piscatorial Association, while gliders from a nearby club float serenely above. The ford, no longer fordable, is an ironically peaceful spot.

One who did succeed in escaping across the Trent was Lord Lovell, a rebel leader. Centuries later his skeleton was discovered mysteriously walled up and sitting at his desk in Minster Lovell, the family home.

A more prosaic fate awaited young Lambert Simnel. He was put to work in the kitchens of Henry VII.

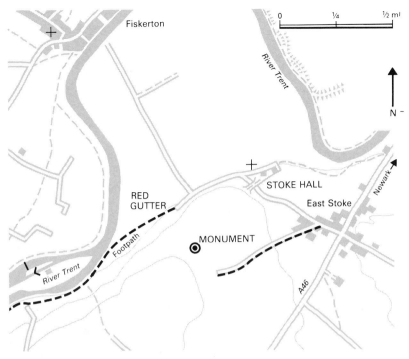

From the meadows beside the river, the land rises to the position held by Lincoln's men. It was down this hill that they were forced to make their disorderly flight.

Part of the battlefield at Stoke is spoiled by the A46 Newark to Leicester road, but the most picturesque area is accessible only by foot. Driving south from Newark on the A46, turn right into School Lane opposite the Pauncefote Arms in the village of East Stoke. This road leads past Stoke Hall to the River Trent, where a ford once offered the only escape for Lambert Simnel's rebels. Fiskerton is the village across the water.

For a pleasant walk along a public footpath in the fields immediately behind the rebel lines, return towards the village and park where the road turns sharp left. A path leading to the right from the elbow of the road takes you past the steep woods which conceal the Red Gutter. In this narrow gully hundreds of Simnel's men died, while others struggled across the fields to the river. This path follows the Trent for about two miles, an enjoyable ramble in summer but not recommended in wet weather for those without suitable footwear.

On your return, just before reaching the A46, turn right up the lane to the hill where the rebels awaited the advance of King Henry. This road turns to gravel and peters out before it reaches the top, but you can still get a good idea of the advantageous position held by Lincoln's army and sense the menace of the sharp drop on the river side of the hill.

A tiny memorial, surely the most obscurely situated (and unseen) battle monument in Britain, is in a hedge about 300 yards from the edge of this track. Since it is on private land, ask permission (and directions) at the nearby farm.

The Battle of Flodden

Since the tenth of September 1513, when rumours of a great calamity first spread through the streets of Edinburgh, the Battle of Flodden has exerted a fascination over historians and poets on both sides of the border. In just two hours of an autumn afternoon Scotland had lost its greatest nobles and churchmen – earls, bishops and abbots. But above all these it had lost James IV, the popular king who had led his infantry into battle and fallen alongside 9,000 fellow Scots.

Although he dabbled in both astrology and the black arts, James could not possibly have predicted such a disaster when he deployed his army along Flodden Hill on the ninth of September. In the two and a half weeks since invading England his army had captured four castles and met with only token opposition. James had no serious designs against England. His brother-in-law, Henry VIII, was at war in France. Obliged by his treaty with the French to take arms against England, James raised a very large

The Battle of Flodden was fought near Branxton, a Northumberland village four miles south-east of the Borders town of Coldstream. The A697 is the nearest main road.

War	Anglo-Scottish Wars.
Date	9 September 1513.
Principal commanders	English: Thomas Howard, Earl of Surrey. Scots: King James IV.
Size of armies	English: About 26,000. Scots: About 30,000.
Duration	From 4:15 to 6:15 in the afternoon.
Outcome	Defeat of the Scots and the death of King James.
County	Northumberland.
Ord. Survey	1:50,000 map no. 74.
Nat. grid ref.	NT 8937.

army to show willing, then proceeded to do very little damage, as if to show where his heart was. He was a complicated man, a patron of science and art, yet obstinate and addicted to the old-fashioned art of jousting. Now the English, commanded by the aged Thomas Howard, Earl of Surrey, and his son the Admiral Thomas Howard, had formally requested a battle on the ninth of September. James accepted the date but replied that he would fight where he wished. As the English assembled near the village of Branxton, James, high on Flodden Hill, was just where he wished to be. Before Surrey's army could fully establish its position, the Scots appeared above them and only 600 yards to the south on the dominating ridge of Branxton Hill.

All might have gone well if James's left flank, a semi-disciplined band of bordermen, had not broken under the English cannon fire and impatiently charged at the Cheshire infantry of Edmund Howard, another of the Earl's sons. They met at first with little oppo-

sition. Perhaps because of this initial success, James himself with the Earl of Crawford ventured from his invulnerable position. It was a fatal mistake. James's army was equipped with the cumbersome fifteen-foot pikes then fashionable in France. Inexperienced in the use of these weapons and slowed down by the marshy ground at the foot of Branxton Hill, the Scots floundered before the bombardment of the Admiral and his father, then fell by their thousands in hand-to-hand combat, their pikes chopped to pieces by the English bills, short pole-arms that were infinitely more effective than pikes at short-range.

While watching this slaughter in the field below, the Earls of Argyle and Lennox, who had remained behind on the Scottish right flank, suddenly found themselves ambushed by Sir Edward Stanley, who had arrived late on the field and climbed up the slippery east slope of Branxton Hill (his men took off their boots to get better footing). In minutes the battle was over. The king's

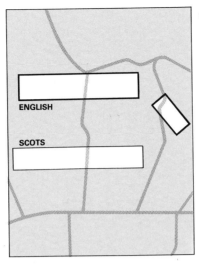

The Scots, encamped on Flodden Hill on the eve of the battle, had a commanding view of the land to the north. Directly ahead of them, in the middle distance below, were the bare slopes of Branxton Hill, the position they assumed on the ninth of September immediately before the fighting began. Branxton, the English position, is hidden by the hill.

body, naked and mutilated, was found in the mire the next day and laid in Branxton Church.

Flodden Field was wild and roadless in 1513. Now it is a patchwork of crops, hayfields and pastureland. Branxton Hill Farm, commanding the left centre of the Scottish line, stands directly above a modern granite monument on Pipers Hill, the position once held by Admiral Thomas Howard. Below that is Branxton Church, restored and enlarged since the battle, though it still scarcely looks adequate to receive *"the slain of both nations"*, as it claims to have done. The village of Branxton, once overrun with English soldiers, is a peaceful spot today. Less than a quarter mile along the narrow road to the south is the low wet ground where the Scots and their king lay all that night.

Beside Branxton in a brook
Breathless they lie,

wrote a contemporary poet,

Gaping against the moon
Their ghosts went away.

Flodden Field is one of the easiest battle-fields in Britain to find. From the A697 Wooler to Coldstream road it is well sign-posted, the monument on Pipers Hill being the centre to which you are directed. Once you are there, however, aside from a book-let in the church, little attempt is made to explain the events of the battle. Here is an itinerary that may enhance your visit:

Take the A697 from Wooler towards Coldstream. After passing through the village of Milfield (about six and a half miles) turn left on a secondary road in 300 yards. Go straight across the B6352. The road now climbs up the ridge of Flodden Hill, where the Scottish army encamped the night before the battle. From the crest of this hill there is a beautiful view of the rolling farmland to the north. In the foreground is the ridge of Branxton Hill, the position the Scots assumed on the day of the battle. Follow the road downhill, turn right at the T-junction and then immediately left. In 600 yards you are at the crest of Branxton Hill in the right-centre of the Scottish line, approximately the point where James him-self stood. To your left and slightly behind you is Branxton Hill, now the site of a farm, from which James's left flank impetuously charged at the beginning of the battle. The Earls of Argyl and Lennox occupied the fields, now partly wooded, to your right.

Continue down the road towards the village of Branxton. This is the steep hill (slippery with mud that September day) which the king and the Earl of Crawford descended to meet the English. The little brook at the bottom of the hill was sur-rounded by a marsh in 1513, a death trap for the Scots with their awkward pikes. Just before reaching Branxton you pass through the position of the English left wing, com-manded by the Earl of Surrey. Turn left at Branxton and left again, keeping the church on your right. The battle monument stands to the left of the road on Pipers Hill. From here there is an excellent view of the entire field. This was Admiral Thomas Howard's observation point. The fields to your right as you face Branxton Hill were the only scene of Scottish success.

Don't neglect to visit the church, which was the grim repository of hundreds of corpses on the day after the battle.

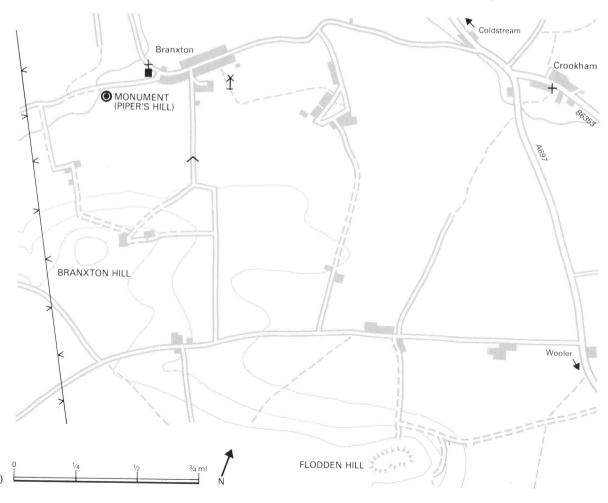

The modern battle monument stands on Pipers Hill, a steep rise to the north of the field near Branxton. This position was held by the English army.

After the battle. the tiny church at Branxton became a mortuary for the dead of both nations (below)

The Battle of Ancrum Moor

So accustomed was Henry VIII to having his way with women that when the Scots showed no interest in the marriage of the infant Queen Mary to Prince Edward, his six year old son, Henry embarked on a ruthless campaign against Scotland. In 1544 the Earl of Hertford, with orders *"to declare and shewe the force of his Highnes sworde to all such as sholde make any resistance unto his Grace's power"*, began the brutal border raids that became known as *"the rough wooing"*.

Cattle were stolen (including 12,492 sheep); crops, towns, castles and churches were destroyed; and men and women were murdered or imprisoned according to the caprice of the invaders. The effect of this policy, however, was not to force the Scots into submission but rather to unite them against the English and to throw them into closer league with France. Even those Scottish nobles who had initially favoured England in the dispute changed sides as these barbarities awoke a dormant strain of nationalism. One such was Archibald Douglas, Earl of Angus, who had lived in England for fifteen years and was considered an intransigent turncoat by his countrymen. Yet on the twenty-seventh of February 1545, he waited on a hill above Ancrum Moor in command of a small Scottish army. Below him, laden with booty, was an English force led by Sir Ralph Evers and Sir Brian Latoun. They were returning south to their base in Jedburgh, having pillaged the town of Melrose, where they had defaced the tombs of the Douglases, Angus's ancestors, thus compounding the hatred of their one-time friend.

Angus knew that to meet the English in open battle, especially an army that outnumbered his by nearly four to one, would be disastrous. He therefore feigned a retreat, withdrawing his men just over the summit of the hill now called Gersit Law. The English generals, familiar with this Scottish tendency to avoid pitched battles, decided to force an issue, and rode hard towards the point they had last seen the Scots. On reaching the top of the hill, they were met by the blinding rays of the setting sun and, in an instant, by the full force of the Scots, who had been awaiting the English advance in battle formation.

The actual battle was over in a matter of minutes. With pikes and broadswords the Scots forced the breathless and astonished Englishmen off the hill and into a hasty retreat. This

Ancrum is in the Borders Region of Scotland, four miles north of Jedburgh on the B6400.

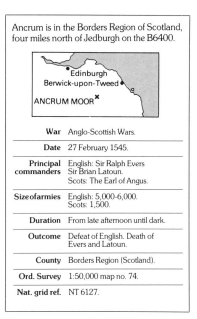

War	Anglo-Scottish Wars.
Date	27 February 1545.
Principal commanders	English: Sir Ralph Evers Sir Brian Latoun. Scots: The Earl of Angus.
Size of armies	English: 5,000-6,000. Scots: 1,500.
Duration	From late afternoon until dark.
Outcome	Defeat of English. Death of Evers and Latoun.
County	Borders Region (Scotland).
Ord. Survey	1:50,000 map no. 74.
Nat. grid ref.	NT 6127.

A Victorian mausoleum stands on the summit of Gersit Law. In 1545 a Scottish army lured the English up these slopes by feigning retreat. The resulting engagement was a convincing Scottish victory, but only a temporary setback for the English, who continued their "rough wooing".

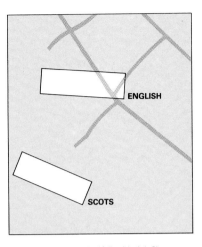

The lichen-spotted tomb of Lilliard (right). She was a Scotswoman whose lover had been killed by the English and who rode to her death at Ancrum Moor.

became a panic when 700 borderers, who had been reluctantly serving with the English, turned on their masters in the bloody pursuit across Ancrum Moor. Until nightfall the rout continued. Evers and Latoun fell alongside 800 of their men; at least 1,000 others were imprisoned. And what a February night in enemy country held in store for the English stragglers is not recorded. The Scots claimed only three casualties. Even given a natural tendency on the part of the victors to underestimate their losses, the Battle of Ancrum Moor was undoubtedly one of Scotland's great triumphs against the English.

Henry VIII did not, as a result of this defeat, change his ways and "woo" more gently, but he died in 1547, having failed to win a Scottish daughter-in-law. At the Battle of Pinkie he took posthumous revenge.

Ancrum Moor is two miles north of Ancrum on the A68. Walks from either side of this main road give long views and a clear impression of the battlefield.

From Ancrum drive north towards Melrose on the A68. In about a mile and a half the road begins to climb, fringed on the left by a long plantation of conifers. Just before reaching the summit, pull off at a track on the left. This leads through the woods up to Gersit Law, the summit of which is crowned by a gloomy mausoleum built in 1864. It was from here that the Scots saw the English returning from the northwest after another successful raid on the border country. It still serves as an excellent viewpoint for all directions except the north-east, where Ancrum Moor itself is obscured by the plantation. It is likely that the Scots withdrew in battle formation to the gentle slopes just to the south-west of Gersit Law, out of sight of the English. When the English army reached the summit they discovered a bristling welcome of pikes and axes.

The ensuing battle spilled over the summit of Gersit Law and down across Ancrum Moor, the Scots in pursuit of the English. Return to the main road and continue up towards the top of the hill for seventy-five yards. A gate on the right leads across Ancrum Moor to Dere Street, a Roman road leading north-west to south-east and a probable route of the English army on their way from Melrose. Dere Street still crosses Ancrum Moor, its relentless way marked by an unswerving avenue of beeches. Just before Dere Street intersects the moor, a crumbling and overgrown monument of red sandstone marks the grave of Lilliard, a heroine who rode to her death with the Scottish army after her lover had been killed by the English.

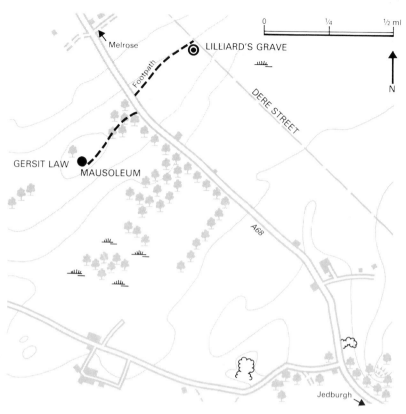

Upon the English loons she laid many thumps,

says a grotesque verse on the tomb,

*And when her legs were cuttet off
She fought upon her stumps.*

Two more sad lines refer to the tomb:

*By me it's been mendit,
To your care I commend it.*

Jedburgh Abbey (right), a few miles south of Ancrum Moor, was a conspicuous victim of English border raids. In his campaigns of 1544-45, Hertford sacked the city of Jedburgh and reduced the abbey to a ruin.

Dere Street (below) is now a grassy avenue of beeches. The English were likely returning along this route when they were surprised at Ancrum Moor.

85

On a plain south of Musselburgh (right) the Scottish schiltrons, close formations of pikemen, were mowed down by devastating fire from the English artillery.

The Battle of Pinkie was fought near Musselburgh in the Lothian Region of Scotland. Musselburgh is on the A1, five miles east of Edinburgh.

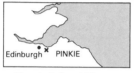

War	Anglo-Scottish Wars.
Date	10 September 1547.
Principal commanders	English: The Duke of Somerset. Scots: The Earl of Arran.
Size of armies	English: About 16,000. Scots: About 25,000.
Duration	From 8 a.m. until midday.
Outcome	Defeat of the Scots.
County	Lothian Region (Scotland).
Ord. Survey	1:50,000 map no. 66.
Nat. grid ref.	NT 3671.

The Battle of Pinkie

The death of Henry VIII in January 1547 did not relieve Scotland of the muscular diplomacy that had typified his reign. Edward VI, a boy of only nine years old, was nominally king of England, but another Edward actually ruled the land. Three years earlier Edward, Earl of Hertford had laid waste vast areas of the lowlands at King Henry's orders. Now, as Duke of Somerset, Protector of England, he prepared to invade on his own account. His cause was the same: to force the Scots into agreeing to a marriage between King Edward and Mary, their five-year-old princess (later known as Mary Queen of Scots).

Again the Scots refused. Their country was still suffering from the recent wars, and plague had swept the eastern towns, but the Earl of Arran ordered every man between sixteen and sixty to assemble at Edinburgh with one month's food. Wearily the people obeyed.

On the eighth of September the army of the Duke of Somerset drew up on a ridge that runs from north to south seven miles east of Edinburgh overlooking the River Esk. The right flank stood near the sea, where a powerful English fleet prepared to bombard any exposed Scottish manoeuvres. From Falside Hill, the centre of the line, Somerset could see the massive army of the Scots on the west bank of the River Esk. Between them stretched a treeless plain more than a mile wide. On this plain, the day before the battle, there occurred a senseless skirmish in which the small Scottish cavalry was almost completely destroyed by a larger English force. It did not go unnoticed among superstitious Scots that this ill omen occurred on the anniversary of the disastrous Battle of Flodden.

Last minute negotiations came to nothing; both sides restated their positions. And Somerset haughtily refused the challenge of single combat against

86

Falside Castle (below) is visible on the ridge to the east of the battlefield. This high ground provided a strong position for the English immediately prior to the battle.

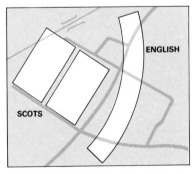

the fiery Earl of Huntly. So on the morning of the tenth of September, the English advanced down Falside Hill with the task of attacking across a river an army nearly twice their size.

Historians agree about what happened next, but no one quite knows why. From their impregnable defensive position the Scots inexplicably began an attack of their own, crossing the river by a bridge at the north of their line and a ford at the south. This was exactly what Somerset had desired. He was superior in both cavalry and cannons, and an open field favoured both these forms of attack. First, though, he had to break up the dense schiltrons formed by the Scots. These were close formations of pikemen, their weapons extended in a fearsome bristly mass – described by one Englishman as *"the skin of an angry hedgehog"*. Somerset's heavy cavalry bore down on these formations with predictable results: horses disembowelled, riders impaled and the schiltrons still intact. But cannon balls were not so easily stopped by men with long sticks, and when the

English artillery opened fire, the dense crowds of pikemen fell like skittles. The chaos in the Scottish line was compounded by the fact that many of the Highlanders, alarmed by the roar of gunfire, escaped to quieter (and safer) spots before they had seen any action. Others stopped to loot the dead English horsemen and then left the field with their plunder. To make matters worse, a sudden shower of rain made the visibility so poor that one band of Scots turned on another, mistaking them for Englishmen.

The Battle of Pinkie was one of the worst defeats ever suffered by the Scots. Apart from a few hundred men lost in the early stages of the battle, the English suffered few casualties, while 10,000 or more Scots died, many in frantic retreat across the River Esk.

The tenth of September became known to Scots as Black Saturday, but it was best described by the English contemporary Patten: *"deadly, lamentable, furious, outrageous, terribly confuse, and so quite against the quiet nature of man"*.

87

The battlefield of Pinkie is now partly covered by the buildings of Musselburgh, Wallyford, and Inveresk but the English position on Falside Hill is still open land with a splendid view and is the best place to start your visit. From Musselburgh drive east towards Tranent on the A1. In about three miles turn right on a secondary road marked Birsley Brae. This leads up Falside Hill and roughly follows a line a little behind the English army from right flank to left as they drew up the day before the battle. Just past the summit of the hill is Falside Castle, now a private house, which was the approximate centre of the English line before their advance. From the little lane beside the castle is an excellent view of the flat

fields where much of the fighting took place. Though they are now crossed by roads and a railway, there is still much open farmland. Beyond is the River Esk, which the Scots so rashly crossed to do battle. Arthur's Seat still dominates the middle distance. Continue on past the castle and turn right down the hill, following the advance of the English army. At the bottom turn right on the main road and then left at a lane leading to a sewage treatment plant. This cuts across the centre of the battlefield, now monotonously flat farmland. A walk along the track that leads left in 300 yards gives a good idea why this terrain was ideally suited to the English cavalry and artillery. From here Falside Hill dominates the landscape.

Inveresk Church stands on a little hill to the east of the River Esk. At the time of the battle this was open land overlooking the Scottish position on the opposite bank. The English were intending to occupy it when the Scots attacked. Now buildings obscure the view of the river.

The Scottish position is almost entirely built over, but it is worth visiting the river, where so many Scots lost their lives, especially to see the sixteenth-century bridge (now for pedestrians only) that stands 200 yards upstream from where the A1 makes its noisy crossing.

A view west from the English position on Falside Hill (below). The plain in the middle distance is the battlefield. Arthur's Seat dominates the horizon.

A sixteenth-century stone bridge spans the River Esk at Musselburgh. The Scots abandoned their position on the west of the river in order to meet the English.

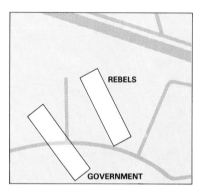

The Battle of Wrotham Hill

The only suggestions that Blacksole Field has a military ancestry are the serried rows of apple trees in the orchards of New House Farm, and a street called Battlefields Road in an adjoining housing estate. Otherwise it is a tranquil spot, forgetful of the time when Kent was a centre of Thomas Wyat's short-lived rebellion.

Wyat was the son of the courtier and poet Sir Thomas Wyat, but he inherited little of his father's charm and prodigality. He was an able soldier, a man of principle and a patriot whose implacable hatred of Spain led to his insurrection and death. Enraged at Queen Mary's intentions to marry Philip II of Spain, he was easily recruited to join a conspiracy. When his fellow plotters confessed or withdrew, he alone continued to rebel, alarming the men of Kent with tales of an imminent Spanish invasion.

On the morning of the twenty-eighth of January 1554, 500 rebels led by Sir

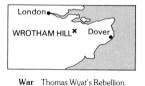

Wrotham (pronounced Rootam) is in Kent, ten miles west of Maidstone, just south of the A20 and M20 London to Folkestone roads.

War	Thomas Wyat's Rebellion.
Date	28 January 1554.
Principal commanders	Government: Henry Neville (Lord Abergavenny). Rebels: Sir Henry Isley.
Size of armies	Government: About 3-400. Rebels: 500.
Duration	Less than an hour in mid-morning.
Outcome	Defeat of the rebels.
County	Kent.
Ord. Survey	1:50,000 map no. 188.
Nat. grid ref.	TQ 6059.

Henry Isley were marching from Sevenoaks to reinforce Wyat at Rochester. Believing they had avoided a pursuing Government force led by Lord Abergavenny, the party proudly raised their pennons and started up Wrotham Hill in high spirits. This was their undoing. Lord Abergavenny and a few of his fellow horsemen saw this conspicuous display of bravado and rushed upon the rebels, cutting them off at Blacksole Field. It was one of the least valorous encounters in English history. Isley's men, who outnumbered their attackers and had the hill in their favour, could manage only a few shots with their long bows before retreating as fast as possible. Many were killed or captured, and Sir Henry Isley, according to an unsympathetic contemporary, *"lay all that night in the wood and fled into Hampshire."*

The rebellion ended a month later with Wyat's imprisonment. Blacksole Field has been quiet ever since.

The wooded slopes of Wrotham Hill (left) as seen from the west, the direction of the rebels' advance. After the rout Sir Henry Isley "*lay all that night in the wood*".

Southwards towards Borough Green are the level fields (above), over which Lord Abergavenny rode in his spectacularly successful attempt to intercept the rebels.

To reach Blacksole Field, turn north up Wrotham High Street, passing the church on your right. Then bear left on the Old London Road, pass the school and immediately turn left again on the Pilgrims' Way. In a short distance this becomes a track. Blacksole Field slopes down to the left just beyond the housing estate.

Although it is safe to assume that a conflict as disorderly as that at Wrotham Hill spilled far in each direction, the area known as Blacksole Field today is a rectangular plot roughly 500 yards east to west by 400 yards north to south. It is bordered on the north by the Pilgrims' Way and on the west by

New House Lane, a track leading down to New House Farm. Both of these are public rights of way; the field itself is private land.

Wrotham Hill is a mile to the north-east of Blacksole Field. From the roundabout at the junction of the A20 and the A227 a path leads up to the summit that Isley's rebels never attained. From the top is a fine view of the rolling, wooded land to the south.

Yaldham Manor, where Lord Abergavenny first sighted the rebels of Sir Henry Isley, is two miles west of Wrotham. A modern house in the days of the rebellion, it still offers a glimpse of its Elizabethan chimneys from Kemsing Road.

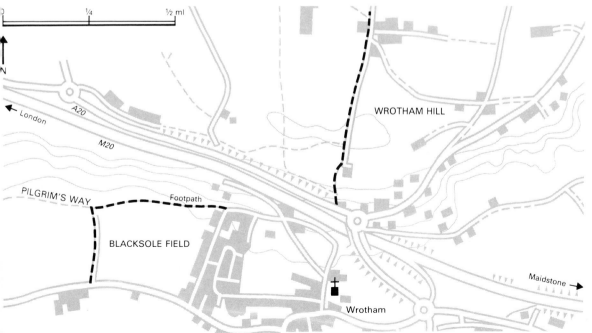

The Battle of Stratton

Stamford Hill stands 250 feet above the sea in north-east Cornwall. To the north the land dips then rises again to form a ridge running parallel with the coast. To the south and east the slopes are steep and partly covered by woodland and the houses of modern Stratton. The western fields fall away gradually through pastureland to meet the ocean at the resort town of Bude. On the grassy summit is a curious earthwork. It is shaped like a horseshoe, the open end facing east, as if the man who built it could conceive of no threat from that precipitous side. For the Earl of Stamford, leading a well-equipped Parliamentarian army into Cornwall, this hill was an ideal defensive position, just the place to put an end to Sir Ralph Hopton's struggling western campaign.

Stamford was not a renowned general. He has been criticized for adopting such a defensive strategy when Hopton's army was only half the size of his and low on both ammunition and rations. Hopton himself put a brave face on his problems, claiming that men and officers alike *"were all very well contented with a dry biscuit apiece"* on their advance to Stratton two days before the battle. This spartan menu was the same the next day, however, and at a council of war on the evening of the fifteenth of May it became clear to the Royalists that if they did not fight a battle immediately they would not be fit to fight one at all. Accordingly, at first light on the morning of the sixteenth of May, Hopton divided his infantry into four parties, keeping 500 mounted men in reserve, and advanced up the hill. Whether by accident or design, the inexperienced Earl of Stamford had the Royalists exactly where he wanted them.

Most of the fighting took place on the south and west of the hill, Hopton himself leading one of the attacking groups. Beside him, on the long western slopes, was Sir Bevil Grenville, a popular commander whose family home was very near Stratton. Two days of nothing but biscuits and water seem to have taken none of the spirit out of the Cornish infantry. All morning and well into the afternoon they tried repeatedly to gain the summit and the earthworks, but the Parliamentarian defenders, aided by thirteen cannon, continued to repulse them.

At three o'clock Hopton learned that less than four barrels of powder remained. Keeping this crisis to himself and his officers, he ordered his men to advance with swords and pikes, firing only upon reaching the summit. It is a tribute to their discipline and courage that they obeyed his bizarre instruction, advancing silently against the firepower of the Parliamentarian army. This madness so unnerved the defenders that in panic they began to scramble down the hill (well behind their leader, the Earl of Stamford, some unkind historians have suggested). James Chudleigh, the young Parliamentarian general, tried to rally his men by leading a charge, but his capture a few minutes later effectively ended the battle, and by four o'clock the four Royalist parties had met jubilantly on the summit. Sir Ralph Hopton, a man who knew a miracle when he saw one, persuaded his exultant army to join him in a prayer of thanksgiving. *"In that fight,"* he wrote, *"God blessed the Royalist's party."*

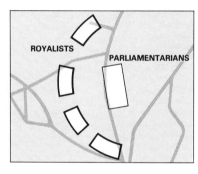

ROYALISTS   PARLIAMENTARIANS

Stratton is a village on the A39 in Cornwall. It is a mile east of the coastal town of Bude.

The flat summit of Stamford Hill (above) seemed an impregnable position to the Parliamentarian defenders.

War	The Civil War.
Date	16 May 1643.
Principal commanders	Parliamentarians: The Earl of Stamford James Chudleigh. Royalists: Sir Ralph Hopton.
Size of armies	Parliamentarians: 5,600. Royalists: 2,900.
Duration	From 5 a.m. until about 4 p.m.
Outcome	Defeat of the Parliamentarians.
County	Cornwall.
Ord. Survey	1:50,000 map no. 190.
Nat. grid ref.	SS 2207.

The battlefield of Stratton is an easy and rewarding site to visit. All the action centred around the ancient earthworks on the summit of what is now called Stamford Hill (after the defeated commander). Driving south along the A39, turn right for Poughill on a secondary road in the town of Stratton. This leads up the south slope of Stamford Hill, reaching the summit in a quarter mile. Immediately beyond the entry to Bevil House, just where the road begins to level off, is a little green gate in the hedge to your right. This leads to the field and the fortifications held by James Chudleigh and his confident Parliamentarian army. A modern plaque and a knobbly obelisk mounted on an archway commemorate the battle. Thick woods on the steep eastern slope of Stamford Hill obscure the view in that direction, but to the west is a beautiful prospect of the sea and the town of Bude.

For a pleasant (if rather unrevealing) tour of the western slopes, scene of much of the fighting continue along the road past the summit, turning left on a gravel track in 200 yards. Turn left again in a quarter mile on a lane which follows the contours of the hill back to the road. These were the slopes up which Sir Bevil Grenville and Sir Ralph Hopton led their men in repeated assaults.

In the town of Stratton is the Tree Inn, a striking building which dates from the sixteenth century and served as Grenville's headquarters prior to the battle. In the courtyard is an enormous portrait of the enormous Cornishman Anthony Payne, a valued assistant to Grenville.

The eastern slopes of Stamford Hill (below) were too steep to encourage a Royalist attack from that direction.

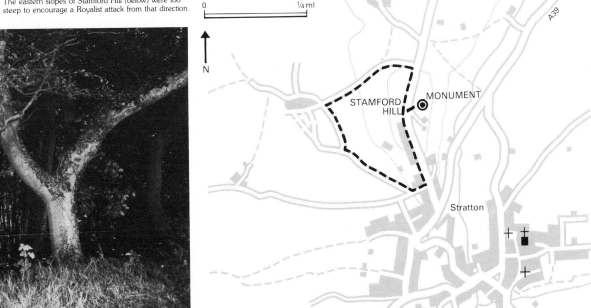

The Battle of Chalgrove Field

The fame of Chalgrove Field derives solely from the reputation of one man: John Hampden.

Hampden was a Parliamentarian politician of exceptional ability and integrity. Far better known than his first cousin Oliver Cromwell in the early years of the war, he had steadfastly defied the king in matters of taxation, and in 1627 had spent a year in prison for refusing to pay a trifling sum. In the early months of 1643 he was, for many, the only man likely to reinvigorate the floundering Parliamentarian efforts. Although not an experienced soldier, he was the popular candidate to succeed the indecisive Earl of Essex, Commander-in-Chief of the Parliamentarian army.

Hampden had no such ambition. In June 1643 his chief aim was to persuade Essex to make a determined assault on the Royalist army at Oxford. From this city Prince Rupert, the king's dashing nephew, whose name alone had an hypnotic effect upon Parliamentarian officers, continually harrassed the countryside in lightning raids. On the seventeenth of June he made one such audacious sortie, sacking the town of Chinner, which was only four miles from the Parliamentarian headquarters and the sleeping Essex. By dawn on the eighteenth he was well on his way back to Oxford when he discovered that a smaller and faster group of Parliamentarian cavalry was pursuing him. Sending a party on ahead to secure the bridge at Chiselhampton, Rupert wheeled about and faced his pursuers at Chalgrove Field.

The Roundheads charged through a cornfield and were cut down like corn by a fusillade and countercharge from Rupert. Hampden, wounded in the shoulder, rode from the field in great pain, *"his head hanging down, and resting his hands upon the neck of his horse"*. Essex's army, a mile behind, failed to reach the scene in time and Rupert rode triumphantly back to Oxford.

Chalgrove Field still grows corn, though an airfield and new buildings impinge on the western edge. Hampden's monument is a lichen-covered obelisk erected in 1843 amid great local celebrations. It stands at a crossroads overlooking the field where Hampden received his mortal wound.

Hampden survived only six days after the battle. A story of uncertain authenticity but of undoubted verisimilitude attributes to him these last words: *"O Lord save my country. O Lord be merciful to . . ."*

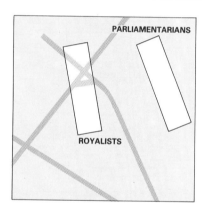

Chalgrove Field is near Chalgrove, a village on the B480 in Oxfordshire, ten miles southeast of Oxford.

War	The Civil War.
Date	18 June 1643.
Principal commanders	Parliamentarians: John Hampden. Royalists: Prince Rupert.
Size of armies	Parliamentarians: About 300. Royalists: 1,000 to 1,500.
Duration	Probably no more than an hour.
Outcome	Defeat of the Parliamentarians and death (six days later) of Hampden.
County	Oxfordshire.
Ord. Survey	1:50,000 map no. 165.
Nat. grid ref.	SU 6497.

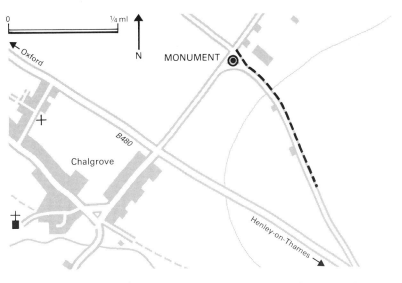

The field at Chalgrove is just that – in summer a gentle, sloping field of grain, very much as it appeared in 1643. Driving towards Oxford along the B480, turn right for Warpsgrove instead of left into Chalgrove village. In just over a quarter mile this lane leads to a cross-roads and the Hampden monument, a squat obelisk which commemorates the death of the popular Parliamentarian leader. Turn to the right here, on a road indicated as a dead-end. In about 200 yards on the left, beyond a depressing poultry farm, is Chalgrove Field itself. Hampden's men charged recklessly down this slope and encountered a fearsome welcome from Prince Rupert and his cavalry, deployed in a line which likely stretched to both sides of the monument.

Driving straight through the cross-roads will take you along Prince Rupert's position but will offer little except a chance to see a second battery farm – Hampden Farm.

The monument to John Hampden (above) commemorates the popular Parliamentarian leader. Hampden was a first cousin of Oliver Cromwell.

Lapwings wheel above Chalgrove Field. In 1643, as today, the battlefield was under cultivation. Hampden's men made their charge across a field of grain.

The Battle of Lansdown Hill

On the morning of the fifth of July 1643 Sir William Waller could have surveyed his position with understandable pride. Having deployed an army of 7,000 along the northern edge of Lansdown Hill, he was admirably placed to defend the city of Bath from a Royalist force led by Sir Ralph Hopton. After weeks of uncommitted skirmishing in the west country, the two armies were at last poised for battle, and Waller had out-manoeuvred his opponent. Behind him stretched the summit of Lansdown Hill, a plateau that extended perfectly level for two miles before falling steeply into Bath. In front of him, to the north, the fields plunged sharply into a valley and then climbed up the formidable slopes of Freezing Hill. If Hopton and his men intended to dine in Bath that evening they would have to show an utter contempt for life and common sense.

The Royalists that morning were in Marshfield, four miles north-east of Lansdown Hill, and were alerted to their enemy's presence by a sortie of horsemen sent to harrass them. Driving this irritating band ahead of them, they moved forward over Tog Hill to a point (possibly the summit of Freezing Hill) from which they could inspect the Parliamentarian position.

Hopton was a brave, not a foolhardy, general. Discovering that his old friend William Waller (the two corresponded affectionately throughout the war while hell-bent on destroying each other's army) had planted himself 250 feet above the valley, he chose to beat a prudent retreat. Waller, piqued at wasting such a splendid position, sent a strong detachment of cavalry down the hill after the Royalists. Though caught from behind, Hopton's Cornish infantry drove the horsemen back and then, at the foot of Lansdown Hill once more and hungry for action, demanded to be allowed the suicidal attack. Hopton acquiesced and arranged his army with infantry on the flanks and cavalry in the centre.

The action was brutal and confused Richard Atkyns, a Royalist cavalry officer who left a vivid account of the battle, wrote that *"the air was so darkened by the smoke of the powder, that for a quarter of an hour together (I dare say) there was no light seen."* Many of the attacking cavalry panicked and fled, believing the battle to have been lost, but the infantry advanced uphill (*"as upon the eaves of an house for steepness, but as unmovable as a rock,"* wrote Atkyns) and at last gained a precarious foothold on the summit.

Stunned by this mad assault, Waller's men withdrew to shelter behind a stone wall a quarter of a mile from their original position. And there, on the hilltop strewn with dead and wounded, the two exhausted armies faced each other, neither strong enough to continue the battle. Scattered sniping continued throughout the night, but shortly before dawn the Parliamentarian army crept back to Bath, leaving their battered victors in sole possession of Lansdown Hill.

Sir Ralph's assault up Lansdown appears as rash today as it did in 1643. The hill is steep enough to make any defending general complacent. From the bottom of Freezing Hill to the top of Lansdown Hill is a daunting enough climb without a hostile army preparing a welcome. The main road down this face is obliged to cut left in a hairpin bend to maintain a decent gradient, but Hopton's men – gallant, foolish, and somehow successful – charged straight ahead. Both sides suffered many casualties. Among the most distinguished men to die was Sir Bevil Grenville, a much beloved Royalist officer, who was struck down upon reaching the summit. A monument dedicated to him stands at the edge of the hill, as if clinging precariously to a hard-won position. On top of it perches a weathered stone griffin, glaring defiantly towards the low wall, where Waller's broken army huddled three and a half centuries ago.

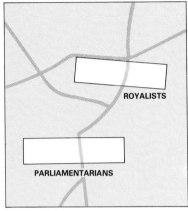

ROYALISTS

PARLIAMENTARIANS

Forced back from their position on Lansdown Hill, the Parliamentarians sheltered behind this wall (above). That night they withdrew to Bath.

A view south along Lansdown Hill. The wall in the distance is the one behind which the Parliamentarians withdrew when the Royalists had struggled to the top.

An interesting way to approach Lansdown Hill is to follow the route of the Royalist army on the fifth of July from Marshfield, eight miles west of Chippenham on the A420, to the battlefield. The village of Cold Ashton, slightly to the south of the main road, is where Waller's cavalry caught Hopton from the rear and provoked him into returning to attack. The A420 then crosses the A46 and ascends Tog Hill, where Sir Ralph Hopton first skirmished with an expeditionary force. Turn left towards Lansdown on the next secondary road (three-quarters of a mile past the

A420-A46 junction). A mile along this ridge at a farm gate, a footpath on the right of the road leads to the summit of Freezing Hill, which is marked by a line of mature beeches. It was here that Hopton made his headquarters. From the southern edge of Freezing Hill you can look across (as Hopton did) to the seemingly impregnable north face of Lansdown Hill, now obscured by trees.

Continue along the road, turning left up through the woods of Lansdown Hill. The monument to Sir Bevil Grenville, marking roughly the centre of the Parliamentarian line, is on the left, just as the road becomes level. A quarter mile farther on is the unassuming stone wall which provided temporary shelter for Waller's army. From a farm track, which runs parallel with this wall and 100 yards behind it, you can reconstruct Waller's last view of the battlefield as

night fell on the fifth of July. Undetected by the Royalists, his men retreated to Bath.

For the walker there is a splendid tour of Waller's left flank and a wonderful view of the countryside to the north. Follow the driveway to the tracking station, that departs from the road opposite the monument. In 400 yards the Cotswold Way, a long-distance footpath, continues along the ridge. This soon emerges on to open land. The view is breathtaking, the Cotswolds rising like a wave above the flat lands of Bristol and the Severn. Freezing Hill, crowned by its soldierly line of beeches, lies to the north-east. At the end of this open ridge there is a trig point and a small wood. Turn sharp right down the hill and follow the farm track to the paved road. Another right turn will take you to the main road and the point where Hopton's men began their laborious climb up Lansdown Hill.

A monument to Sir Bevil Grenville stands on the edge of Lansdown Hill. Grenville, a popular Royalist commander, was poleaxed from his horse upon reaching the summit.

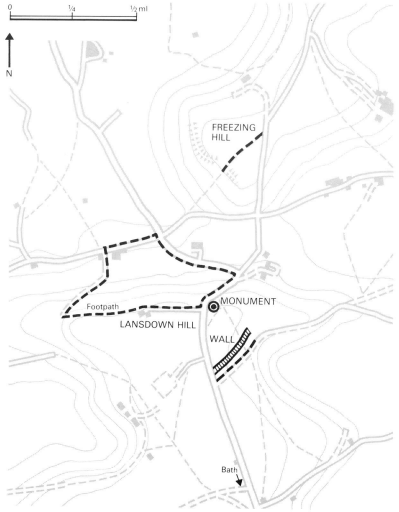

The Battle of Roundway Down

Roundway Down is a broad plateau rising steeply above the Vale of Pewsey to the south and the valley of the River Avon to the west. Gravel tracks and foot-paths criss-cross its surface, and the wide fields of grain create a sense of space that one rarely experiences in lowland countryside.

A scene very much like the one that exists today extended before Lord Wilmot as he led his company of 1,800 horsemen south towards Roundway Down on the afternoon of the thirteenth of July 1643. In those days the land was unfenced and unculti-vated, ideal terrain for an exuberant gallop. But Wilmot and his men were armed for battle and approached cautiously. As they rode down the slopes of Morgan's Hill they saw, as they had feared, a vastly superior force

of Parliamentarian infantry and cavalry barring their way across the centre of the plain. This was the army of Sir William Waller, who had lost to the Royalists at Lansdown Hill just eight days earlier but had nevertheless pursued his enemy and trapped them in Devizes three miles to the south. Waller had every reason to be confident. Sir Ralph Hopton, his arch-rival (and long-time friend), lay in Devizes, blind and immobile from a gunpowder blast. His 2,000 or so Cornish foot soldiers were easy prey for the well-equipped Parliamentarian army. Wilmot's relief force was a desperate measure to relieve a town that was all but captured.

Waller's position was an excellent one. His right flank of cavalry were near the foot of Roundway Hill; his left

under King's Play Hill in the north. In the centre were his 3,000 foot soldiers, and spread along the line were eight guns. In order to reach this formidable barrier Wilmot and his tiny force would have to charge uphill.

What happened next is not entirely clear. Clarendon, a contemporary historian, may have found the right psychological motivation: *"Sir William Waller,"* he wrote, *"out of pure gaiety, departed from an advantage he could not again recover."* He charged with his cavalry down the gentle slope, meeting Wilmot's expert horsemen on equal ground. Within half an hour the action was over. While Waller's infantry and gunners looked on helplessly, unable to fire in case they hit their own men, Wilmot's cavalry savaged their opponents, hounding

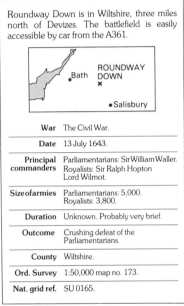

Roundway Down is in Wiltshire, three miles north of Devizes. The battlefield is easily accessible by car from the A361.

War	The Civil War.
Date	13 July 1643.
Principal commanders	Parliamentarians: Sir William Waller. Royalists: Sir Ralph Hopton Lord Wilmot.
Size of armies	Parliamentarians: 5,000. Royalists: 3,800.
Duration	Unknown. Probably very brief.
Outcome	Crushing defeat of the Parliamentarians.
County	Wiltshire.
Ord. Survey	1:50,000 map no. 173.
Nat. grid ref.	SU 0165.

Oliver's Castle, a hill fort on the western edge of Roundway Down. In their panic-stricken retreat, the Parliamentarian cavalry plunged to their deaths on the plain below.

them westward across the down. Neither side was aware of the danger ahead. To the west, with Beacon Hill and Oliver's Castle, Roundway Down ends abruptly in a drop of 300 feet. An observer from the fields below watched while Wilmot's cavalry *"chased them down the hill in a steep place where never a horse went down nor up before"*. Some of the Royalists themselves were unable to stop in time and followed their victims to death on the wrinkled floor of Bloody Ditch.

The rest was easy. Sir Ralph Hopton's men had learned of the engagement and started up the hill from Devizes some time before. When they arrived, they discovered a solitary company of infantry in the centre of the field. Caught between cavalry and infantry, Waller's soldiers suffered a merciless beating.

The shape of the land has changed very little since 1643. Roundway Hill, crowned with a thick clump of trees, still rises to the south-east of the field. King's Play Hill, one of the few areas of pastureland, guards the opposite

corner. Morgan's Hill, at 846 feet the highest land adjoining the battlefield, marks the direction of Wilmot's approach. Very near the centre of the field is Roundway Hill Farm, protected from the north by a close wedge of trees which give it an embattled appearance, as if it is prepared this time for a Royalist attack. The slopes to the south of the field are wooded, but the western approach is as bare and as steep as in 1643. Oliver's Castle and Beacon Hill jut out from the down and tower above the fields to the west. Between them lies the fierce crease of Bloody Ditch, where horses and human beings once tumbled like lemmings to their deaths.

Roundway Down is now a recreation area. An information board tells hikers and picnickers where they may walk or enjoy the view. Children scramble around the steep sides of Oliver's Castle; dogs disappear into fields of barley; but horses, if they exercise that sense for which they are famous, trot prudently along the bridle paths.

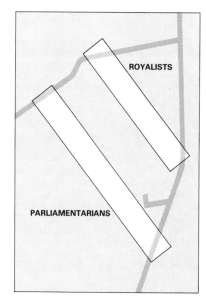

Roundway Down, a treeless plateau, made ideal country for a cavalry engagement. In the early stages of the Civil War, this was a method of fighting at which the Royalists were superior to the Parliamentarians.

The wide summit of Roundway Down provides excellent access to the battlefield for both the motorist and the walker. From Devizes take the A361 towards Swindon, turning left in three-quarters of a mile on a secondary road for Roundway. In just over a mile, after the road has begun to ascend steeply, take a right fork. Where the land begins to level out is the southern edge of the field, a point perhaps 400 yards behind the Parliamentarian position. Cars cannot continue much farther in this direction, as the road becomes too rough, but a walk of three and a half to four miles takes you on a complete circuit of the battlefield. Continue along the straight track. You are facing north, as was Waller's army on the day of the battle. The high land ahead of you is Morgan's Hill. Wilmot's cavalry advanced around its south-east slope. To your right is the wooded summit of Roundway Hill; across the field to your left is King's Play Hill (no association with King Clarles I). These two features indicate the approximate extent of the Parliamentarian line.

Continue past Roundway Hill Farm on your left, with its barrier of trees. The fields ahead were the scene of the first clash be-

tween the opposing horsemen.

At a cross-roads 800 yards past Roundway Hill Farm turn left along a hawthorn-fringed lane. Look left along here to see the field from a Royalist point of view. At Hill Cottage, with King's Play Hill on your immediate right, continue straight, turning sharp left on a rough track in a quarter mile. This is the western edge of the field, the plain over which the Parliamentarian cavalry galloped in their suicidal retreat.

A sharp right in a quarter mile takes you to the car park and information area for Oliver's Castle. It is well worth walking out

on Oliver's Castle, an ancient hill fort unrelated to the Civil War. There are marvellous views of the land to the west, and from the north wall you can look down into the grassy ravine of Bloody Ditch, where hundreds of men and horses fell to their deaths in desperate retreat.

From Oliver's Camp car park a gravel track leads back along the south of the field to join the road from Roundway.

Because of the profusion of paths and possibilities, O.S. map no. 173 is a useful companion on any exploration of this well-preserved battlefield.

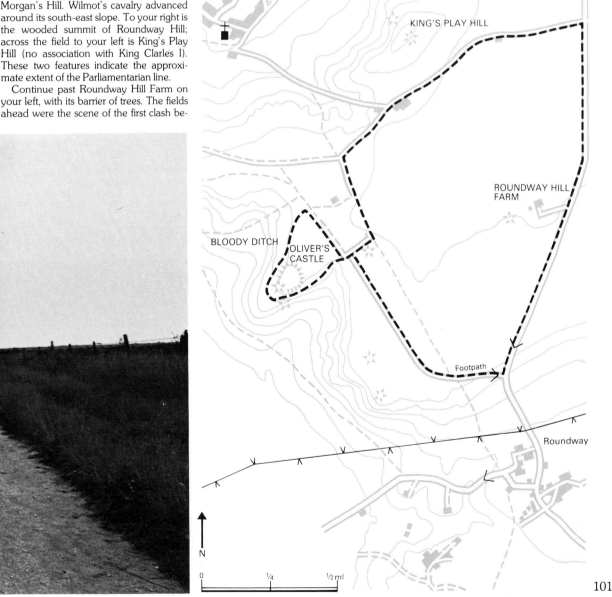

101

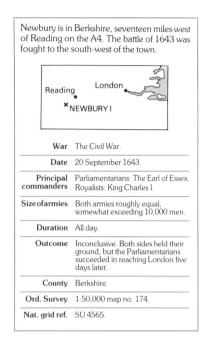

Newbury is in Berkshire, seventeen miles west of Reading on the A4. The battle of 1643 was fought to the south-west of the town.

War	The Civil War.
Date	20 September 1643.
Principal commanders	Parliamentarians: The Earl of Essex. Royalists: King Charles I.
Size of armies	Both armies roughly equal, somewhat exceeding 10,000 men.
Duration	All day.
Outcome	Inconclusive. Both sides held their ground, but the Parliamentarians succeeded in reaching London five days later.
County	Berkshire.
Ord. Survey	1:50,000 map no. 174.
Nat. grid ref.	SU 4565.

The First Battle of Newbury

The First Battle of Newbury confused contemporary historians in much the same way as the elephant confused the blind men in the old fable. Like the elephant it took up a lot of space and consisted of many disparate parts. It was a cavalry charge, an infantry encounter and an artillery duel; it was fought on a plain and a hillside, on open land and among a maze of hedges. At the end of the day no one could claim a victory, though the Parliamentarians held the field and may in retrospect have got the better of the encounter. Today the events of the twentieth of September 1643 are confused even more by the new houses that occupy the south and centre of the field. A modern blind man has only half an elephant to help him define the whole beast.

Certain facts are well established. In early September 1643 King Charles was forced to lift his siege of Gloucester when a powerful relief force under the

Earl of Essex advanced from London. Although thwarted in this campaign, the Royalists were confident that they could defeat the Parliamentarians in a pitched battle. They therefore strove to obstruct the Roundheads on their return to the capital and so to force a fight. On the nineteenth of September Prince Rupert and his cavalry entered Newbury just a few hours before the Parliamentarians, thus depriving them of lodgings. Essex now saw that a battle was inevitable and encamped with his hungry and dispirited army to the south-west of the town. Royalists and Parliamentarians took what sleep they could as they faced each other that night in the wet fields. *"Sometimes,"* wrote a philosophical contemporary, *"looking on the ground, they thought upon the melancholy element of which they were composed, and to which they must return."*

The Royalists would have been better occupied considering the

ground from a tactical point of view. They had failed to take full advantage of their headstart and to occupy all the high land overlooking the Parliamentarian approach. As a result, before dawn the next day the Roundheads marched unopposed up Round Hill on the northern edge of the plateau that rises a mile to the south of the River Kennet. Their line now stretched north-south, from the river on their left for nearly two miles to the open land of Wash Common.

Round Hill, the centre of the battle-field, is now largely open ground, but in the seventeenth century its slopes and summit were criss-crossed with hedgerows. This made it extremely dangerous going for the Royalist cavalry and offered excellent protection for Parliamentarian musketeers. The Royalists, correctly perceiving this as a key position, made repeated attempts to capture Round Hill from the east and north-east. Sir John Byron's

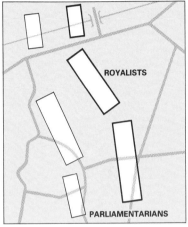

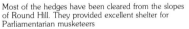
Most of the hedges have been cleared from the slopes of Round Hill. They provided excellent shelter for Parliamentarian musketeers

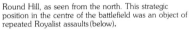
Round Hill, as seen from the north. This strategic position in the centre of the battlefield was an object of repeated Royalist assaults (below).

cavalry and his uncle Sir Nicholas's infantry suffered heavy losses (including the gallant and popular Lord Falkland) in uphill fighting from hedge to hedge. Sir John finally gained and held a foothold on Round Hill but did not succeed in dislodging the dogged Parliamentarian infantry, who now dragged up their cannon and began a devastating bombardment of the centre of the Royalist line.

In the level and more open ground of Wash Common to the south, Prince Rupert and Sir Philip Stapleton had engaged in a series of bloody cavalry charges. The Royalists finally got the better of these encounters but, as on Round Hill, were frustrated by a wall of Parliamentarian infantry. Meanwhile, in the flat fields to the north, by the banks of the Kennet, a series of equally inconclusive engagements resulted in yet another stalemate. *"The night parted them when nothing else could,"* wrote the historian Clarendon, but firing continued until ten p.m.

At midnight the king, alarmed by his shortage of powder, withdrew towards Oxford, and the next morning the Earl of Essex discovered he was unopposed. He instructed the local constables *"to bury all the dead bodies, lying in and about Enburne and Newburywash,"* and continued his battered progress to London.

103

Houses now occupy the southern area of the field at Newbury, but elsewhere the land is still open. The events of 1643 can at least be partly reconstructed.

From Newbury drive south-west along the A343 towards Andover. At the cross-roads in about a mile is the obelisk to Lord Falkland, the most distinguished Royalist casualty. It stands in a little green on the right of the road and asks you to remember Falkland and the Royalists who fell, assuming, perhaps, that the Parliamentarians would look after their own dead. The beloved Lord Falkland did not die here; this monument marks approximately the centre of the Royalist line.

Turn right on Essex Road (a number of the streets in the area have commemorative names) and follow the Royalist advance for a quarter mile to where a foot-path leads off to the right. You are on the broad summit of

Round Hill in the centre of the battlefield. The Parliamentarians succeeded in attaining this elevation before the battle, forcing the Royalists into an uphill assault.

For a circuit of just over two miles, taking you round the northern part of the field, follow the footpath down the slope to the right (in places this is overgrown; bare legs are not advisable). The wide, sloping field to your left was criss-crossed by hedges in 1643. It was up this hill that Sir John Byron's cavalry and the infantry of his uncle Sir Nicholas made their dogged assault. Somewhere along here also, Lord Falkland rode out between a gap in a hedge and was shot down. Keep to the pavement past the modern schools, walk through a corner of a housing estate and turn left along a track thickly fringed by hawthorns. To your right is the flat northern field of battle, bordered by the Kennet, where Sir William Vavasour

attacked the Parliamentarian infantry of Major Fortescue. To your left is Round Hill, which the Parliamentarians defended for so much of the day. Turn left on the paved road and left again up the lane to Essex Road, following roughly the Parliamentarian line of defense. At the cross-roads is Wash Common Farm, which has changed little in three and a half centuries.

Another survivor of the battle is Bigg's Cottage, where the Earl of Essex is reputed to have spent the night of the nineteenth of September. Continue along Essex Road past Wash Common Farm. Bigg's Cottage is the ancient thatched building on the left of the road in about a mile and a quarter.

The Newbury Museum has a model and display of both battles of Newbury. It is open weekdays 10-5 (October to March, 10-4); closed Wednesday afternoons, Sunday and Bank Holidays.

The Falkland monument commemorates one of the most popular Royalist leaders. Lord Falkland was deeply affected by the Civil War. It has been suggested that his death was as much the result of suicidal impulses as of pure gallantry.

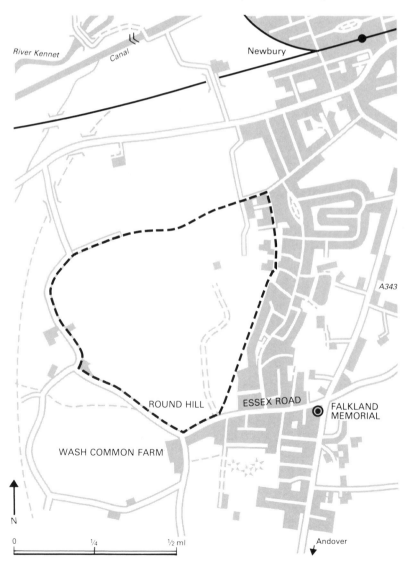

Wash Common Farm, relatively unchanged since 1643, stands in the centre of the battlefield.

The north slopes of the battlefield fall away to the River Kennet. It was up this hill, then criss-crossed with hedges, that Sir John and Sir Nicholas Byron made a laborious advance.

The Battle of Cheriton

Winter is the off-season for warfare in England. Skirmishes and sieges, fierce proclamations and desperate fund-raising continue, but major campaigns often sink to a muddy halt. The spring of 1644 came as something of a relief to both the Royalists and Parliamentarians, each side eager to resolve their uncertain encounters of the preceding summer. On the twenty-ninth of March Sir John Smith, general of the Royalist horse, was especially keen for battle, *"at meat that morning, bidding his soldiers to feed heartily, for they should have princely sport anon"*. What he so joyfully anticipated was another clash between those two fierce rivals (though the best of friends in peace) Lord Hopton of the king's army and Sir

William Waller of Parliament. The purpose of this impending encounter was simple: Hopton, victor at Lansdown Hill, aimed to gain control of south-east England and so prepare the way for an assault on London; Waller intended to prevent him doing so.

On the same morning that Sir John Smith was exhorting his men at their breakfast, Waller, encamped in the fields near the village of Hinton Ampner, moved swiftly to capture a favourable position for battle. He sent 800 men into Cheriton Wood and directed the main body of his army to occupy a ridge that runs east-west from the woods to the village of Cheriton. Facing north on this elevation Waller must have looked with satisfaction on

his early morning manoeuvre. To his right was Cheriton Wood. From it emerged three ridges, each about 600 yards apart – a trident with the prongs facing west. Between the southern-most ridge, where he stood, and the lower central one was a flat open field. Otherwise the slopes were enclosed by hedges, ideal protection for musketeers. Waller would recognize only the shape of the land today; except for the woods, there is no protection among the open fields that cover the entire area.

The Royalists, who had spent the night near Alresford, were quick to respond to Waller's move. Perceiving that the Parliamentarian soldiers in Cheriton Wood posed a threat to the

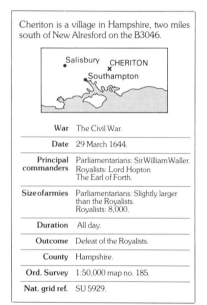

Cheriton is a village in Hampshire, two miles south of New Alresford on the B3046.

War	The Civil War.
Date	29 March 1644.
Principal commanders	Parliamentarians: Sir William Waller. Royalists: Lord Hopton The Earl of Forth.
Size of armies	Parliamentarians: Slightly larger than the Royalists. Royalists: 8,000.
Duration	All day.
Outcome	Defeat of the Royalists.
County	Hampshire.
Ord. Survey	1:50,000 map no. 185.
Nat. grid ref.	SU 5929.

left flank of any position he might logically occupy, Hopton sent a strong force of musketeers to drive them out. There was a fierce battle among the trees until the Parliamentarians panicked and scrambled back to their dismayed army. Hopton, now drawn up along the central ridge, wished to take advantage of this disarray among the Parliamentarians by launching an attack through the newly-captured woods, but the old Earl of Forth advised him to stay and defend. Forth, a doughty (and gouty) champion of distant wars, was nominally Hopton's superior, though he was content to let the younger man take most of the initiative. On this occasion, however, neither man was in total control. With-

out a word of warning, a hot-headed young Royalist on the right flank took it upon himself to start the battle, riding down to the open ground at the foot of the ridge. His party was demolished; those who were not killed were captured. This initial disaster seemed to infect the entire Royalist army. They continued to attack in this hopeless fashion, although they were considerably outnumbered and encountered murderous gunfire from Parliamentarian musketeers behind the hedges at the foot of the south ridge.

How the battle ended is unclear; one contemporary suggests that the Royalist army was outflanked from the right. There is no question that their retreat did them more credit than their

attack. Hopton saved nearly all his heavy guns in withdrawing through Alresford. But he left several hundred men on the field behind him. Worse still, he left a confident Parliamentarian army in control of the field at Cheriton.

Among the dead lay Sir John Smith. His horse, alarmed by cannon fire, had reared sideways, presenting a row of Parliamentarian musketeers with an easy target. Sir John was hit twice. Then *"comes one amongst them clad in arms, like a lobster, who with his carbine gives him his third and mortal wound in the belly . . . With this wound he falls, and with him the fortunes of the day."*

The "princely sport" of civil war had claimed one of its great exponents.

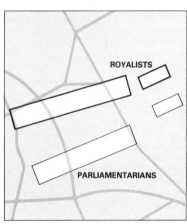

A low ridge in open farmland, seen here from the north-west, marks the position held by the Royalists before the battle.

107

The Battle of Cheriton was fought in the fields immediately to the east of the village. Drive along the B3046 towards New Alresford and turn right on an unmarked secondary road at the north end of the village of Cheriton. In just over a mile you will pass under a power line. Leave your car a few yards farther on, where a farm track hairpins to the right. In 600 yards this track climbs to the Royalist position, a low, sloping ridge running east-west. Ahead of you is the higher Parliamentarian ridge. The flat land between these heights is where most of the confused action took place. Neither Lord Hopton nor Sir William Waller would recognize the cleared fields and long views of the site today. To your left is the dark mass of Cheriton Wood, scene of much tactical skirmishing early in the battle. Continue along this path, skirting the woods in the hollow and climbing the Parliamentarian ridge. Where the land begins to level off, turn right through a gate and follow an undefined right of way along a row of beeches. This leads along the Parliamentarian position and provides an excellent view of the entire field. In half a mile turn right along a farm track, which dips into the valley, ascends the Royalist position and leads to the road about half a mile from where you left your car.

Continue driving along the road away from Cheriton. The modern battle monu-

A line of beeches now occupies the Parliamentarian position. The ridge to the right was in Royalist hands.

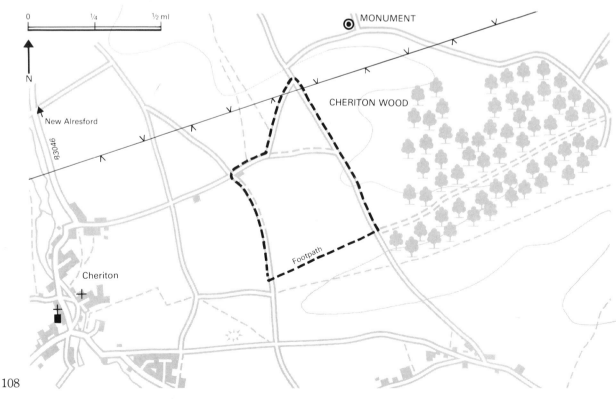

108

ment stands at a quiet T-junction on the left in another half mile. You are now on the northernmost of the three ridges that emanate from Cheriton Wood. To the south is a view of the Royalist position, seen from behind the lines.

Cheriton Wood is private property today, but it is not a particularly reliable historical record, as it has almost certainly outgrown its boundaries of 1644.

This area provides some of the best battlefield walks (or, if you have brought your horse with you, rides) in the country. O.S. map no. 185 suggests a number of attractive paths and bridleways.

A modern stone commemorates the battle, making special reference to the Royalist withdrawal. This was their most successful operation in the campaign.

Daisies spill out across a path on the west of the battlefield. In 1644 the area was overgrown with hedges.

The Battle of Cropredy Bridge

It is easy to imagine the scene at Cropredy on the twenty-ninth of June 1644. On either side of the River Cherwell were two open ridges running north-south. On each ridge, and within plain sight of each other, was an army spoiling for a fight. King Charles led the army on the east bank; Sir William Waller, the Parliamentarian commander, that on the west. For days these two had wandered through the midlands in search of the perfect site for a battle, neither willing to risk an inferior position. At last Waller thought he saw his opportunity. As he looked across the Cherwell to the opposing ridge, he discovered a wide gap developing in the Royalist line. The vanguard and the centre of the king's army had left the rearguard a mile or more behind. With the intention of dividing the Royalists and crushing the two halves separately, Waller sent a strong band of horsemen under John Middleton to take Cropredy Bridge, which was defended by a party of Royalist dragoons. He himself took 1,000 of his men to Slat Mill Ford, about a mile downstream, in order to catch the Royalist army from behind.

Charles had indeed allowed a gap to develop in his army. Hearing that 300 enemy horsemen were ahead, attempting to join up with Waller, he hastened forward to cut them off, leaving his ignorant rearguard strung out along the ridge. His good fortune was in having two remarkable commanders at the rear of his army. The Earls of Cleveland and Northampton nearly single-handedly repelled the Parliamentarian attack. At Slat Mill Ford, Northampton took Waller and his men by surprise with a sudden charge down the hill, and drove them back to the west bank.

The action at Cropredy Bridge was more complicated. Without any diffi-

The village of Cropredy is on the River Cherwell, four miles north of Banbury in Oxfordshire. From Banbury take the A423 for Coventry and turn right for Great Bourton and Cropredy.

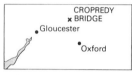

War	The Civil War.
Date	29 June 1644.
Principal commanders	Parliamentarians: Sir William Waller. Royalists: King Charles I.
Size of armies	Parliamentarians: About 6,000. Royalists: About 9,500.
Duration	From 1 p.m. until sunset.
Outcome	Defeat of the Parliamentarians.
County	Oxfordshire.
Ord. Survey	1:50,000 map no. 151.
Nat. grid ref.	SP 4746.

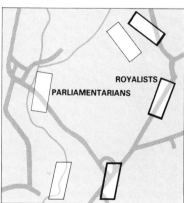

The River Cherwell at Cropredy Bridge. Confident of the protection that the river afforded him, King Charles allowed a wide gap to develop in his army.

culty, Middleton brushed aside the Royalist dragoons and crossed the river. Elated by this easy success, some of his horsemen rode ahead to Hay's Bridge. The Earl of Cleveland, seeing his chance, attacked the Parliamentarian infantry, who "*thought the devil had come upon them in a cloud of dust*" and scrambled back to the bridge. Middleton's cavalry, having been repulsed at Hay's Bridge, were now caught returning by Cleveland and "*necessitated to retreat very disorderly*". The battered Parliamentarians crossed the Cherwell and made no attempt to renew the Battle of Cropredy Bridge.

Cropredy has two bridges now, one spanning the Oxford Canal, the other crossing the Cherwell. To the east are the flat fields over which Middleton's men spilled in their first exuberant attack. The land on both sides of the river is remarkably unchanged. If the ghosts of King Charles and Waller were to attempt a recreation of the battle, they would be able to re-enact the same violence in the same places. Perhaps they are kept at bay by the neglected little plaque on the side of the bridge, with its faint message: From Civil War Good Lord Deliver Us.

The road from Cropredy to Williamscott includes two bridges today, but in 1644 the Oxford Canal was not built and the only water between Sir William Waller and King Charles was the River Cherwell. The bridge from which the battle takes its name has long since disappeared, but the present Cropredy Bridge is in the same place, and commemorates the event with an inscription. From this valley a Parliamentarian force, full of confidence, left the security of the bridge and advanced up the hill to the east towards Wardington. They were eventually beaten back to the river by the Royalist rearguard. Waller himself crossed the river at Slat Mill Ford, about a mile to the south of Cropredy. A foot-bridge now crosses the river at this point. To get there, leave Cropredy on the road to Great Bourton, turning off to the left just before going under the railway bridge. After a quarter mile continue on foot along a public path to Pewet Farm. Turn left on a track past the farm buildings. This leads down to the canal and the river, where the ruins of Slat Mill can still be seen.

For a particularly fine view of the battlefield from the Parliamentarian position, turn right at Pewet Farm and walk up the hill to the Great Bourton-Little Bourton road. To the north and the east you can see the principal area of conflict and the ridge along which the Royalist army was marching.

For the field as the Royalists saw it, cross the bridge at Slat Mill and walk up the hill through the pastures towards Williamscott, the village just above Cropredy. An ordnance map and a bit of luck will keep you on the right of way. There are fine views from these slopes of Waller's position on Bourton Hill.

The Wardington Ash, under which King Charles ate his lunch the day of the battle, no longer stands, but a remarkably solitary ash tree, no doubt a descendant, grows in a corn field on the left of the A361 as you drive from Williamscott to Wardington.

Half a mile north of Wardington the A361 crosses the River Cherwell at Hay's Bridge. Charles and his vanguard had already crossed safely to the hill on the other side when Waller launched his attack at Cropredy and Slat Mill. The Royalists returned and successfully defended this crossing.

O.S. 1:50,000 map no. 151 shows the whole area of battle criss-crossed with rights of way. Not all of these are easy to find, but the visitor does not need to confront angry farmers in order to get an excellent impression of this most accessible of battlefields.

King Charles ate his lunch sitting under an ash tree on the day of the battle. This solitary ash is in the right spot but appears too young to have been so honoured.

The Battle of Marston Moor

The Battle of Marston Moor began in a thunderstorm in the late afternoon; it ended long after sunset, the moonlight silvering 5,000 corpses. It began with the Parliamentarian army facing north, the Royalists south; it ended with the armies reversed, both sides having swung 180 degrees clockwise, in a great seething wheel.

It almost didn't begin at all. So great was the reputation of Prince Rupert that when he arrived with his army to relieve the siege of York, the Parliamentarians withdrew from the city and prepared to block his way on Marston Moor, six miles to the west. Rupert declined the formal offer of battle and took a northern route around this human obstacle, entering the city of York unopposed on the evening of the first of July after a march of twenty-seven miles. The next morning, against

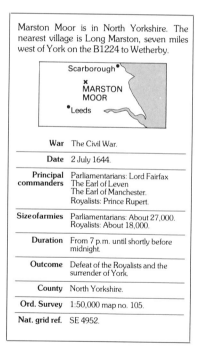

Marston Moor is in North Yorkshire. The nearest village is Long Marston, seven miles west of York on the B1224 to Wetherby.

War	The Civil War.
Date	2 July 1644.
Principal commanders	Parliamentarians: Lord Fairfax The Earl of Leven The Earl of Manchester. Royalists: Prince Rupert.
Size of armies	Parliamentarians: About 27,000. Royalists: About 18,000.
Duration	From 7 p.m. until shortly before midnight.
Outcome	Defeat of the Royalists and the surrender of York.
County	North Yorkshire.
Ord. Survey	1:50,000 map no. 105.
Nat. grid ref.	SE 4952.

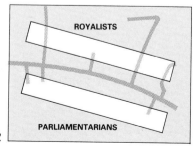

the advice of his ally, the Marquess of Newcastle, he led his exhausted army out again to meet the Parliamentarians on Marston Moor.

The Parliamentarian commanders were not in complete agreement either. After an evening of wrangling they had finally begun to withdraw their troops, with the intention of meeting Prince Rupert farther south, when Rupert suddenly appeared in front of them (or behind them, as only their rear guard now remained on the field). Laboriously, the Parliamentarian army reassembled on the moor. By mid-afternoon both sides were prepared for battle, the Parliamentarians on higher land to the south of the field, the Royalists in a defensive position behind a long dry ditch on the unenclosed levels of Marston Moor. Prince Rupert, normally quick to attack, considered it too late in the day to begin a battle and rode off to his dinner. The Marquess of Newcastle settled back in his coach and lit a pipe. At about seven p.m. he was startled out of his reverie (or his slumbers) by the sound of fighting.

Both armies were spread over a line stretching more than a mile and a half from east to west. As well as they could, the entire Parliamentarian army advanced simultaneously. On the right the cavalry of Sir Thomas Fairfax (later commander-in-chief of the New Model Army) met the cavalry of Lord Goring; on the left a similar engagement occurred between Cromwell and Prince Rupert; in the centre the largely Scottish foot soldiers forced back the musketeers manning the ditch and confronted the Royalist infantry.

Fairfax and 400 of his men succeeded in breaking through on the right, but the rest of his cavalry panicked and fled, some creating havoc among their own infantry. Cromwell was wounded in the neck early on in his engagement (years later, Mark Trevor, esq., who inflicted the sword wound, was made a viscount by King Charles II for this act of heroism) but his "ironsides" eventually drove back the famous Royalist cavalry. Rupert was unhorsed and forced to hide in a bean field. In the centre the Royalist infantry slowly pushed back their attackers. This central success so discouraged Lord Leven, one of the Parliamentarian commanders, that he galloped from the field and didn't stop until he reached Leeds. Lord Fairfax, Sir Thomas's father, was equally dismayed. According to one story, he

rode home and went straight to bed, to be wakened at midnight with the news of victory. Fortunately, the bulk of the Parliamentarian army was unaware of these defections. Cromwell, returning bandaged to the field, chased the Royalists completely around behind the battle to their own left flank until he was facing south, the Royalists (those, at least, who resisted) north. *"God made them as stubble to our swords,"* wrote Cromwell soon after the battle.

Then it was that the superior numbers of the Parliamentarians began to take their toll. Harassed by horse and foot, the Royalist infantry retreated. Newcastle's 3,000 Whitecoats withdrew to a single field and fought until, according to one story, only thirty were left alive.

Marston Moor presents an inexpressive face today, but most of the features

that existed in 1644 are still visible. Cromwell Plump, a gentle hill crowned with a tuft of trees and once head-quarters of the Parliamentarian command, is the only area of any geographical interest. The rest is low, flat land, divided by fences and hedges of thorn. It is easy to understand how the battle turned in a half circle. At night on such a large and undramatic field soldiers would have little by which to orient themselves. It is extraordinary that one side was well enough organized to claim a victory at all.

The plague of civil war did not infect all the inhabitants of Yorkshire that summer. One reassuring anecdote tells how a resident of Long Marston was stopped by a soldier shortly before the battle and asked if he was for the king or for Parliament. *"Whäät!"* said the local, *"Be them two fall'n out then?"*

The featureless plain held by the Royalists in 1644 (above). It is easy to understand how at night in such a landscape the armies became disoriented.

Moor Lane (below) is an ancient track. It was the scene of fighting between the cavalries of Lord Goring and Sir Thomas Fairfax.

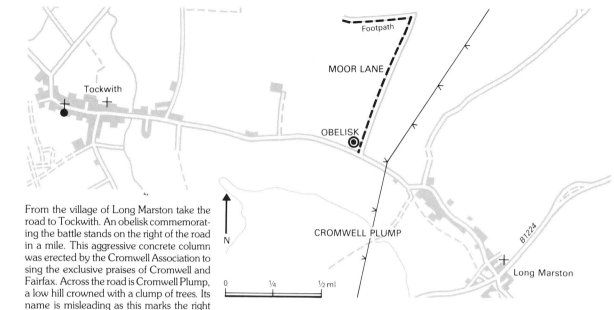

Footpath

MOOR LANE

OBELISK ◎

CROMWELL PLUMP

N

B1224

Long Marston

Tockwith

0   ¼   ½ ml

From the village of Long Marston take the road to Tockwith. An obelisk commemorating the battle stands on the right of the road in a mile. This aggressive concrete column was erected by the Cromwell Association to sing the exclusive praises of Cromwell and Fairfax. Across the road is Cromwell Plump, a low hill crowned with a clump of trees. Its name is misleading as this marks the right flank of the Parliamentarian army, a position commanded by Sir Thomas Fairfax. Cromwell himself was on the extreme left of the line, a mile to the west. Cromwell Plump, which is an excellent viewpoint, is unfortunately on private land and virtually inaccessible.

To the north of the road are the flat fields of Marston Moor, where the Royalist army was stationed. Walk along Moor Lane, a rough track beside the monument. In 1644 this road was in much the same state as it is today. On your right is the scene of the bloody engagement between the cavalry of Fairfax and Lord Goring. A number of Fairfax's men rode along Moor Lane, under fire from Royalist snipers behind the hawthorns. This was also where Oliver Cromwell's cavalry, in the final confused hours of darkness, scattered Lord Gorings's flank from behind.

To your left in about a quarter of a mile is a heavily overgrown ditch, still fringed with thorns, behind which 1,000 Royalist musketeers fired upon the advancing infantry. This was a more significant barrier at the time of the battle, but it is remarkable that it still exists after nearly three and a half centuries. The featureless plain on your left was the centre of the battlefield, scene of a fierce infantry engagement.

Continue on Moor Lane and turn left at the cross-roads. In a quarter of a mile this leads you to the heart of the field, where Newcastle's White Coats died in a stubborn last stand. On a fine day it is a pleasant walk, but the spirit of Marston Moor pervades the entire field and does not demand such a long expedition.

To the south-east of the field is Cromwell Plump (below), an isolated tuft of trees on a low ridge. In reality, Cromwell was nowhere near this spot. He faced Prince Rupert on the western side of the field.

The Battle of Lostwithiel

On the thirteenth of August 1644 the citizens of London were asked to participate in a fast *"to crave a blessing from God on the forces of the Earl of Essex in the west"*. Essex was 250 miles away in Cornwall, outnumbered and surrounded, his army near starvation – in need of every blessing God or Parliament could bestow.

He had entered Cornwall at the end of July, having been persuaded by one of his generals that the populace there would gladly take arms against King Charles. In this he was cruelly misled. Cornwall was among the loyalest counties in England, unlikely to favour an army that had pillaged and plundered its way from Horsebridge to Bodmin. To add to his griefs Essex discovered that he was pursued by a powerful Royalist army led by the king, while approaching him from the west was Sir Richard Grenville and his Cornish army. On the second of August he withdrew to the town of

Lostwithiel is in Cornwall on the A390, eleven miles south-west of Liskeard.

War	The Civil War.
Date	31 August 1644.
Principal commanders	Parliamentarians: The Earl of Essex. Royalists: King Charles I.
Size of armies	Parliamentarians: About 8,000. Royalists: Unknown, but outnumbering the Parliamentarians.
Duration	All day.
Outcome	Surrender of Parliamentarians.
County	Cornwall.
Ord. Survey	1:50,000 map no. 200.
Nat. grid ref.	SX 1054.

Lostwithiel on the River Fowey, fully expecting supplies to arrive by sea from Plymouth and reinforcements to attack the king from the east. He waited all month. Steady westerly gales prevented relief from the ocean, while his last hope of help by land vanished when the small army of Sir John Middleton was defeated in Somerset.

Meanwhile the Royalists closed in with merciless efficiency. They captured ruined Restormel Castle immediately to the north of Lostwithiel, Druid's Hill to the north-east and Beacon Hill to the east. They occupied the ports to the south-west and placed strategic outposts along the east bank of the River Fowey. Essex was restricted to a narrow strip of land five miles north to south, two miles wide. *"And now the King's forces had a full*

By seizing strategic positions around Lostwithiel, the Royalists forced the Parliamentarians to retreat towards the sea. Restormel Castle fell early in the campaign.

prospect over all the others' quarters,"
wrote the historian Clarendon. For
Essex it was like living in a box with
contracting walls and a glass roof.

On the misty night of the thirtieth of
August Essex ordered his 2,000
cavalry to squeeze through the enemy
lines and retreat eastwards. Despite the
fact that the Royalists had been forewarned, this desperate plan succeeded. Early the next morning Essex
led his infantry out of Lostwithiel in the
only direction left to him – southwards
towards Fowey – hoping that a similar
stroke of luck would bring the long-
awaited relief ships that very day from
Plymouth. The Royalists, watching the
town from Beacon Hill as a cat watches
a fish pond, were down in an instant.

All that morning and much of the
afternoon the Parliamentarians staged
a brilliant fighting retreat, battling their
way backwards from hedge to hedge.
Once or twice they recovered land with
unexpected sorties, but for every two
fields they captured they fell back
three. By early evening they were defending the strongest position available
to them: the ancient earthworks of
Castle Dore which command the ridge
from Lostwithiel to Fowey.

In 1644 this stronghold was barri-
caded all around by hedges. Today it is
relatively exposed, revealing the precarious situation into which the Parliamentarians had been forced. To the
east and west the fields slope rapidly
away into land held by the enemy. To
the north is the ridge along which the
Royalists advanced. Behind is the sea,
which must have looked a cold and
doubtful haven. They got no farther
that evening. There was some brief
skirmishing and an exchange of
cannon fire (one shot landed within
twenty yards of King Charles as he ate
his supper in a field), but the damage
had been done. The Parliamentarian
right flank had given way and the
Royalists had streamed down behind
them to Fowey. Castle Dore was surrounded, its occupants starving and, as
they soon discovered, leaderless. The
Earl of Essex had slipped away by sea
to Plymouth when it became apparent
that all was lost. (*"I thought fit to look to
myself,"* he wrote.)

The next day Major-General Philip
Skippon negotiated surrender terms
with King Charles, and 6,000 bedraggled soldiers left for the east. They
suffered terribly from cold, hunger,
disease and from the remorseless men
and women of Cornwall along their
route. Fewer than 200 died in the
Battle of Lostwithiel; more than 2,000
lost their lives on that long march to
Dorset.

Castle Dore (above), an Iron Age hill fort, lies on the
ridge between Lostwithiel and Fowey. It was here that
the Parliamentarian infantry made their last stand.

Even if the Parliamentarian army had succeeded in
reaching the coast at Fowey (below), they would have
received a rude welcome from Royalist cannon.

Like a game of chess, the Battle of Lost-withiel was a series of manoeuvres which eventually compelled one side to concede. The endgame occurred at Castle Dore, an Iron Age fort, where the Parliamentarian army, deserted by their commander-in-chief, laid down their arms.

From Lostwithiel take the A390 to St. Austell. In about two miles turn left on the B3269 to Fowey. Castle Dore is on the left in three miles, just past the entry to Lawhibbet Farm and concealed from the road by hedges. The B3269 is busy and narrow (as the Earl of Essex complained of its ancestor in 1644) and is not safe for parking, but the owner of Lawhibbet Farm, on whose land the castle stands, permits considerate visitors to leave their cars along the track. The castle occupies an excellent defensive position, dominating the ridge from Lostwithiel, along which the Royalists inexorably advanced.

Opening Royalist moves in this military chess game surrounded the Parliamentarians in Lostwithiel and gradually cut off their means of retreat. Sir Richard Grenville easily captured Restormel Castel, one mile

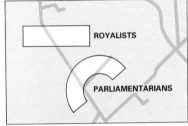

ROYALISTS

PARLIAMENTARIANS

north of Lostwithiel. Its picturesque ruins are well worth a visit. From Lostwithiel it is clearly sign-posted along a secondary road. Mid-March to mid-October it is open 9:30-8:30; Sundays 2-6:30. Winter hours are 9:30-4; Sundays 2-4. There is a small admission charge.

Two other strategic points above Lostwithiel, Druid's Hill and Beacon Hill, were also captured by the Royalists. You can get an idea of just how vulnerable a town Lostwithiel was by looking down on it from the latter position. Leave Lostwithiel on the A390 for Liskeard. In about half a mile turn right, then fork immediately left up Beacon Hill. From the T-junction at the top you can see the town below, caught between the steep walls of the river valley.

The Royalists also attempted to seal off all escape routes by water to the south. The Bodinnick Ferry at the mouth of the River Fowey was one such position they controlled. The B3269, which passes Castle Dore, leads directly to Fowey where a ferry provides the only route for vehicles to the eastern bank. No longer threatened by Royalist cannon on the far shore, Fowey is a pleasant spot to visit.

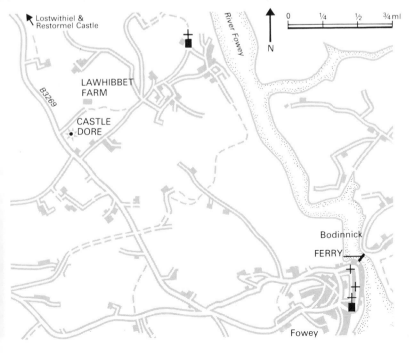

Lostwithiel & Restormel Castle

River Fowey

N

0   ¼   ½   ¾ ml

LAWHIBBET FARM

B3269

CASTLE DORE

Bodinnick

FERRY

Fowey

117

The Second Battle of Newbury

The battle fought at Newbury in 1644 was not a straightforward confrontation between two armies. It was a confusing series of engagements complicated by topography, poor communications, miscalculation, shared command, hesitation, tortuous tactics and finally by darkness. And in the end no one was really sure who had won. The Parliamentarian forces woke up on the morning following the battle to find themselves in sole possession of the field and of the town of Newbury, but the two great buildings around which fighting had raged the previous day, Donnington Castle and Shaw House, were still in Royalist hands, and King Charles was on his way to Oxford.

Donnington Castle was a major reason for a battle being fought in the first place, and it is appropriately from its ruins that the visitor gets the best impression of the field. Only the tower of the gatehouse stands today, an improbably slim structure without the walls and turrets that the besieging Parliamentarian army grew to know so well during the Civil War. It was described by Camden in 1586 as "*a small but very neat castle seated on the banks of a woody hill*", and so it still

appears. The village of Donnington, just below the castle to the east, is untouched by the sprawling advance of Newbury. Looking south one can see through the trees to the little River Lambourn, which once protected the king's right flank. On the other side of the water is open farmland, the northern-most fringe of the battlefield. It is flat, pleasant land, shared by grain and by cattle, with moorhens bustling along the edge of the stream. In 1644 this area was threatened by the cannons of Donnington Castle, a consideration which may have discouraged Oliver Cromwell from making a resolute contribution to his flank of the battle. Beyond these open fields are the red brick residences of Newbury and Speen, now permanently encamped in the centre of the action.

Shaw House, the other major Royalist fortification, is just over a mile to the east of Donnington Castle. It appears now, as it appeared 300 years ago, a gracious Elizabethan mansion with broad windows and a welcoming drive, but it was the scene of ferocious combat in the late afternoon and early evening of the twenty-seventh of October. Now a school, the only evi-

dence of its military past are the high earthworks which protect the house from the north and east and the cannon barrels which lie on the pavement by the front door in order to define parking spaces for senior staff.

The battle was complicated partly by design, partly by mischance. Royalist troops, led by the king and his nephew Prince Maurice (younger brother of Prince Rupert), advanced victoriously out of Cornwall in the autumn of 1644. Hoping to lift the siege of Basing House, near Basingstoke, they were thwarted by a huge Parliamentarian army of 19,000, the combined forces of the Earl of Manchester, the Earl of Essex and Sir William Waller. In the face of such opposition, the king chose to relieve the gallant Colonel Boys at Donnington Castle, north of Newbury. Heavily outnumbered, he nevertheless fixed upon a strong position, establishing his headquarters at Shaw House, then the residence of a Mr Dolman.

When the Parliamentarian troops assembled on Clay Hill and surveyed the Royalist fortifications a mile to the west, they decided against a direct assault. A council of officers chose instead to surprise the enemy from

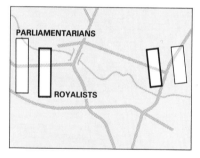

The Second Battle of Newbury, one of the most confusing events of the Civil War, was further complicated by the River Lambourn (right), which flowed through the middle of it.

behind. They divided their forces, leaving Manchester in command of Clay Hill and sending two-thirds of the army on a thirteen-mile night march north around the Royalist position. The surprise failed totally, as the king had been forewarned. When the Parliamentarian army finally arrived at the village of Speen in mid-afternoon of the twenty-seventh of October, they met a Royalist force, this time facing west, under the command of Prince Maurice. Their initial attack was successful but, under the vigilant guns of Donnington Castle, the Royalists staged a brave counter-attack.

Meanwhile, on the eastern front, Manchester had been slow in mounting an attack, a move which was intended to coordinate with the Speen offensive. When he finally did advance he encountered stubborn and deadly resistance on the embankments and in the gardens of Shaw House.

Darkness finally made it too dangerous to continue fighting. *"It was now night,"* wrote the historian Clarendon, *"for which neither party was sorry."* Nor was either party much the wiser as the Second Battle of Newbury drew to an obscure close.

Newbury is in Berkshire, seventeen miles west of Reading, on the A4.

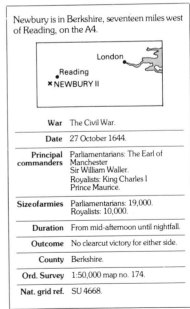

War	The Civil War.
Date	27 October 1644.
Principal commanders	Parliamentarians: The Earl of Manchester Sir William Waller. Royalists: King Charles I Prince Maurice.
Size of armies	Parliamentarians: 19,000. Royalists: 10,000.
Duration	From mid-afternoon until nightfall.
Outcome	No clearcut victory for either side.
County	Berkshire.
Ord. Survey	1:50,000 map no. 174.
Nat. grid ref.	SU 4668.

Donnington Castle stands on a hill to the north of the battlefield. Throughout the Civil War it remained in Royalist hands, paying dearly for its resistance. The dark patch on the left tower indicates where bricks have been used to repair damage made by cannon.

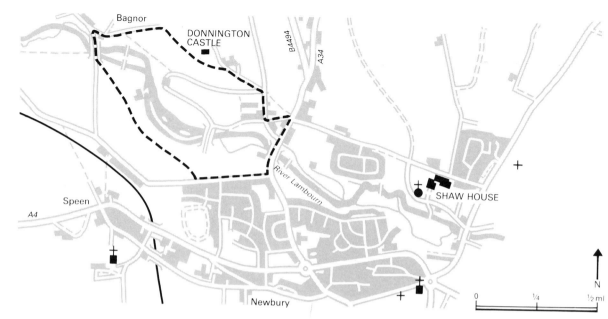

The battlefield of Newbury itself does not allow the visitor any long rambles. Roads, water, fences and houses bar his way. But there is plenty to see. Donnington Castle is an attractive ruin and provides an excellent view of the western front of the battle.

From the A4 take the B4494 north towards Wantage for nearly a mile. Turn left to Donnington village and follow signs to the castle. From among the ruins on the hilltop, look south across the River Lambourne. Speen and Newbury now occupy most of the battlefield, but the fields immediately across the river give a flavour of 1644. For a walk of about two and a half miles through Castle Woods and the northern part of the field, take the footpath which turns right at the castle car park as you face downhill. Follow it to the village of Bagnor, turn left at the main road, cross the River Lambourn and go over the stile across the fields to your left. This is the Parliamentarian left flank, an area which lay within range of the Donnington guns. The path leads to Grove Road. Follow this left to the B4494 and thence back to the castle.

Leaving Donnington Castle, turn left on the B4494 and then immediately right for about a mile. After crossing over the A34, turn right. Shaw House, now a school, is the mansion on the left past the church.

Newbury museum has a display devoted to the Civil War and the town's two battles.

Shaw House, occupied by the Royalists, was the scene of a confused nighttime skirmish. The Parliamentarians were forced to withdraw.

The fields to the south of Donnington Castle, on the other side of the River Lambourn (above), were where the heaviest fighting occurred. Neither side emerged a clear-cut victor.

Much of the battlefield is now obscured by the houses of Newbury and Speen. The banks of the Lambourn are an exception.

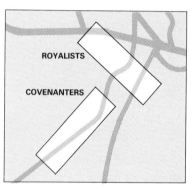

The Battle of Auldearn

In the spring of 1645, while the fortunes of King Charles I floundered towards disaster at the Battle of Naseby, the Royalist cause in Scotland was prospering under the inspirational leadership of James Graham, Earl of Montrose. Since the previous autumn he had won a series of daring encounters – at Tippermuir, Aberdeen and Inverlochy – always against much larger armies, while in between engagements he spirited his men across Scotland with what seemed supernatural speed.

Montrose, a nobleman and an accomplished poet, was accompanied on these dazzling campaigns by Alasdair MacDonald, his perfect foil. MacDonald (or MacColla, as he was often known) was a massive Irish warrior, a gaelic chieftain who inspired his followers with blind devotion and his enemies with terror. The 1,000 soldiers he had brought with him from Ireland were especially dreaded after their savage spree of murder, rape and looting at Aberdeen, a Covenanter stronghold that had made the mistake of resisting in September 1644.

In early May 1645 Montrose and MacDonald camped in the village of Auldearn near the south shore of the Moray Firth. Eighteen miles to their west, in Inverness, was the Covenanter force of Major-General John Hurry. Montrose's small army was outnumbered nearly two to one, but such odds no longer alarmed the Royalists, and both sides prepared for an imminent battle. Hurry, who had fought for the Royalists a year before at Marston Moor, was the first to move. As if determined to prove that Montrose was not the only daring tactician in Scotland, he set out towards Auldearn on the evening of the eighth of May with the intention of surprising the Royalists in a pre-dawn attack. This was not a bad plan, for Montrose had grown complacent in his meteoric career. *"The raine was very vehement all that night,"* wrote a contemporary, and the Royalist scouts were *"too confident that there was no danger."* Unfortunately for the Covenanters, Hurry and his men were also affected by the poor weather. Concerned that their powder was getting wet, they dis-

charged their muskets at what they thought was a safe distance from Auldearn, but the gunshots flew northeastwards with the wind and alerted half a dozen Royalist scouts, who raced back to camp.

For much of the Battle of Auldearn, only a quarter of the Royalist's small army was actually in action. Alasdair MacDonald, alerted by the scouts, managed to rouse about 500 men. Dispersed behind fences and protected by marshy ground to the west of the town they formed a north-west to south-east line, a frail defence against Hurry's army that was now bearing down on them. They nonetheless fought desperately, playing for time while, still behind the line, Montrose assembled the main body of his army. Goaded into rashness by this hopeless task, Alasdair even launched an attack of his own, but his men became caught in the very bog that had previously protected them. Disaster was averted when a cavalry detachment of only 100 men galloped from behind the town and broke through the right flank of Hurry's army; another, under Lord

Auldearn is in the Highland Region of Scotland, two miles east of Nairn on the A96.

War	The Civil War.
Date	9 May 1645.
Principal commanders	Covenanters: Major-General John Hurry. Royalists: The Earl of Montrose Alasdair MacDonald.
Size of armies	Covenanters: About 4,000. Royalists: About 2,000.
Duration	Unknown. From first light.
Outcome	Defeat of the Covenanters.
County	Highland Region (Scotland).
Ord. Survey	1:50,000 map no. 27.
Nat. grid ref.	NH 9155.

Garlic Hill (above) to the south-west of Auldearn. General Hurry's attack on the Royalists took him along what is now the B9101 to the east of the hill.

The fields to the west of Castle Hill are still swampy in wet weather. This marshy land greatly impeded the Covenanters' nighttime attack on Montrose at Auldearn.

Gordon, then dashed at the Covenanter's left flank. And at last Montrose was ready with the bulk of his infantry and advanced through the town to reinforce Alasdair. Hurry's army, unable to make use of its superiority in numbers because of the wet ground, a hill and the narrow column in which it had been forced to advance, was shattered by this three-pronged attack. The Royalists showed no mercy. Alasdair's men, who knew that they faced a Campbell regiment, attacked their traditional enemies with a violence well beyond the call of duty. The rest of the Royalist army found other grievances to justify the extreme brutality of their counter-attack. *"Remember Donald Farquharson and James of Rynie,"* they shouted, referring to men recently murdered by the Covenanters.

Their revenge was thorough. Few of Hurry's soldiers straggled back to Inverness that evening; nearly 3,000 lay stripped and mutilated in the wet fields to the south and west of the town.

Although he had literally been caught napping at Auldearn, Montrose won two more battles that summer, becoming a legendary figure in the process, the king's one remaining hope for victory in the Civil War.

123

The Battle of Auldearn was fought immediately to the west and south of the modern village. From Nairn drive east along the A96 towards Elgin. At Auldearn (about two miles) turn left on a road signposted to the Boath Dovecote. This leads to Castle Hill from which there is a commanding view of the plain to the west. (The Dovecote, or Doocote, a seventeenth-century palace for pigeons, stands in the middle of the field on the summit.) From here you get an excellent idea of the terrain on which the fighting took place.

There are several contemporary accounts of the Battle of Auldearn, and yet there is much that is left unsaid or that is actually contradictory. The traditional description of the battle is one pieced together by S.R. Gardiner, a Victorian historian whose version has gone unchallenged until very recently. Gardiner ignores the element of surprise in the Covenanters' attack and claims a brilliant tactical victory for Montrose – a story suggested by Montrose in his own account. This version, which has Montrose and a concealed detachment of Royalists ambush General Hurry in a devastating flank attack, is the one presented on the excellent battle display board which stands on Castle Hill.

An alternative version, convincingly developed by David Stevenson of Aberdeen University (and presented in the brief history here), makes Montrose a much more fallible leader. This has Hurry advancing along the route of the B9101, which leads south-west from Auldearn and was the main road from Inverness in the seventeenth century. Auldearn was then a tiny hamlet running north-south rather than east-west along the present A96 as it does today. On their sodden night march the Covenanters would have been forced into a column between Garlic Hill (now pastureland immediately south-west of Castle Hill) and the low wooded ridge to its east. It is easy to imagine how Alasdair MacDonald and his small band could have defended the village for some time before Hurry's much larger army had completely arrived at the scene. In his defence Alasdair was aided by marshy land between the town and the advancing Covenanters. This still creates a natural barrier in the field immediately to the west of Castle Hill.

Montrose was very likely stationed at Boath House, a quarter mile north-east of Castle Hill. His army, although encamped nearby, would doubtless have taken a considerable time to call to arms in the confusion of the damp dawn. When Montrose and the Royalists finally entered the battle in full force, the fighting spilled out across the fields to the west and south of Auldearn. Houses as far apart as Kinnudie (half a mile west) and Kinsteary (nearly a mile south) are mentioned in contemporary accounts as scenes of the ensuing slaughter.

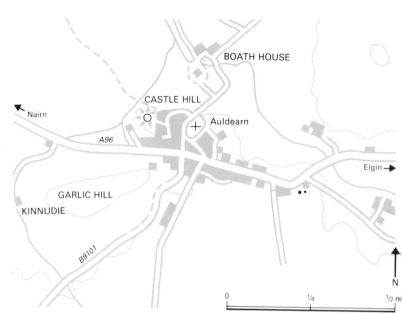

Sheep and cattle share the slopes of Garlic Hill on a quiet summer evening.

The fields to the south and west of Auldearn were strewn with the corpses of Covenanters, cut down while retreating to Inverness.

A monument (left) stands near the centre of the Parliamentarian line. Both armies occupied high land, but neither had any positional advantage.

Naseby is in Northamptonshire, seven miles south of Market Harborough. From Northampton take the A50 for Leicester and in twelve miles turn right to Naseby on the B4036.

The Battle of Naseby

The visitor to Naseby soon learns that he is in the geographical centre of England. From this little village, he is told, waters flow both east and west, two rivers, the North Nene and the Avon, claiming Naseby as their source. But the area is central to England in other ways. It is England as celebrated in pictorial calendars and sentimental verse: rolling farmland chequered with fields; hedges of thorn, rose and holly. One gets the feeling that there is still roast beef on the tables of Naseby.

The battle fought just north of the town in 1645 was also central, though its effects were far from reassuring to the England of John Bull. An obelisk erected north-east of the village in 1823 to commemorate the battle (though not, strangely, on the field itself) gives the reaction of the Fitzgeralds, Lord and Lady of the Manor, still appalled after nearly two centuries at what could happen in their England. This battle says the inscription, "*led to the subversion of the throne, the altar and the constitution and for years plunged the nation into the horrors of anarchy.*"

Another monument, on a ridge more than a mile to the north, is less assertive. It claims to be near the spot where Oliver Cromwell led his cavalry against the struggling left flank of the Royalist army. Cromwell was actually considerably to the east of this point, but the monument is the best place to appreciate the positions of the opposing armies in what was the most decisive battle of the Civil War. Looking north, one sees the land slope down to the flat fields of Broadmoor (where Broadmoor Farm now stands) and then rise gently to a parallel ridge less than a mile from the monument. It was there, on Dust Hill, that King Charles and Prince Rupert prepared for battle. Their army stretched for about a mile, from somewhere beyond Prince Rupert's Farm on the left (as one sees it from the monument) to Long Hold Spinney, the dense woodland on the right. In those days the land was unenclosed and only partly cultivated. The Royalist army, though heavily outnumbered, were eagerly awaiting battle. They had every confidence that with a brisk charge across the open valley of Broadmoor they could panic the untried recruits of Sir Thomas Fairfax's New Model Army, who lined up opposite them on Red Hill Ridge.

It was ten in the morning. Both sides had spent the previous few hours manoeuvring from ridge to ridge for a favourable position. Now, at such close quarters, a battle was inevitable. King Charles must have realized how crucial the ensuing hours would be to his dwindling fortunes, but he allowed the twenty-five year-old Prince Rupert to adopt the same enthusiastic tactics that had typified so many of his battles. The Royalists advanced and, true to form, Rupert's cavalry, though under fire from a line of dragoons in Sulby Hedges on the Parliamentarian left flank, forced back the cavalry of Sir Henry Ireton. In the centre the experienced Royalist infantry also at first prevailed, but they were slowly overwhelmed by the sheer weight of men that Fairfax threw at them. Some of Ireton's cavalry had resisted Rupert's attack and rode in to aid their battered infantry. They were reinforced by the dragoons who now emerged from Sulby Hedges, and finally by the cavalry of Oliver Cromwell, who had totally defeated the Royalists on the steep ground of the east side of the field. Rupert's men were meanwhile a mile behind the Parliamentarian line, too distant and too tired to be of any

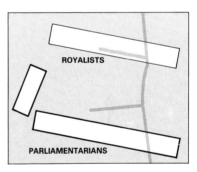

assistance. The king, from his central position on Dust Hill, watched helplessly as his army was crushed and his cause lost.

The contours remain the same, but there are few landmarks now on this tranquil field to assist the visitor in re-creating the battle. Sulby Hedges, where the Parliamentarian dragoons were stationed, are not visible from the monument. Cromwell's commanding position on the Parliamentarian right flank is still evident, but years of cultivation have tamed the rough land below, where he dispersed the king's cavalry. The levels of Broadmoor still show signs of their marshy past, but it is the future that now threatens the field of Naseby. An east-west motorway is poised to vandalize the battlefield more permanently than armies ever could. 127

A view south (above), from the Royalist position on Dust Hill. The road descends to Broadmoor, then climbs to the low ridge held by the Parliamentarians.

War	The Civil War.
Date	14 June 1645.
Principal commanders	Parliamentarians: Sir Thomas Fairfax Oliver Cromwell. Royalists: King Charles I Prince Rupert.
Size of armies	Parliamentarians: About 14,000. Royalists: About 7,500.
Duration	10 a.m. until soon after midday.
Outcome	Defeat of the Royalists and the effective end of the First Civil War.
County	Northamptonshire.
Ord. Survey	1:50,000 map no. 141.
Nat. grid ref.	SP 6880.

The battlefield at Naseby is today bisected by the little road from Naseby to Sibbertoft. For the visitor this is no bad thing, for the roadside provides good views, and private farmland otherwise restricts public access to much of the site.

From Naseby village take the road to Sibbertoft. In just over a mile a short footpath to the left leads to a battle monument, situated at a point to the right centre of the Parliamentarian line. In 1645 the ridge half a mile to the north (Dust Hill) was crowded with Royalist soldiers. King Charles's line stretched from Long Hold Spinney, the woodland on the right, to well past Prince Rupert's Farm on the left.

Next walk north along the road to the entrance of Prince Rupert's Farm. From here you get a good view of the Parliamentarian position as seen by the Royalists. The high ground immediately to the left of the road ahead was occupied by Oliver Cromwell. Broadmoor, the flat land between the two ridges, was a scene of much of the fighting. Hedges, trees and farms have interposed since the Civil War.

Sir Thomas Fairfax, the Parliamentarian

general, did not place all his men in a straight line facing the enemy. Colonel John Okey and his 1,000 dragoons were deployed along Sulby Hedges, a wide stand of trees and shrubs at right angles to the extreme left of the Parliamentarian army. This hedge, now more an overgrown avenue, could still shelter a company of dragoons. It is best seen from the Naseby to Welford road on the right, just past Naseby Hall. Across the fields near here, considerably behind the Parliamentarian lines, Prince Rupert led his cavalry in their unfortunate charge.

Two other sites associated with the battle are the memorial obelisk a quarter of a mile from Naseby on the Market Harborough road (well away from the battlefield) and the Naseby Parish Church. In the north aisle of the church is a table, originally from a Naseby tavern, at which a Royalist party were drinking when they were surprised and captured by a Parliamentarian patrol.

The Naseby Battle and Farm Museum, in the town of Naseby, is open from Easter to the end of September, week-ends and Bank Holidays only, from 2-6.

This obelisk, standing nearly a mile from the battlefield, was erected by a local landowner. *"The subversion of the throne, the altar and the constitution."* it claims, resulted from the defeat.

A table in the church at Naseby. A group of Royalist soldiers are reputed to have been sitting drinking at it in a Naseby tavern when they were captured by a Parliamentarian patrol (above).

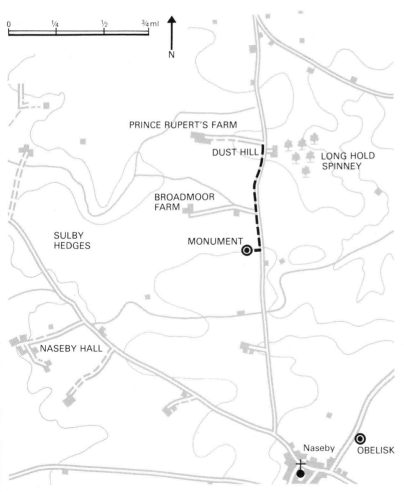

The Battle of Alford, fought a mile to the west of the modern town, is easy to envisage. From Alford drive towards Lumphanan on the A944. In just under a mile a secondary road to the left leads up Gallowhill, where Montrose awaited the Covenanter advance from across the River Don. There is an excellent view of the entire field from a bench on the side of the road at Ardgathen, a cluster of houses 200 yards up Gallowhill. (The bench is probably not for the sole use of battlewatchers. It offers a splendid view of the river valley and the bald moors beyond.) You are now slightly in front of the Royalist line and looking down towards the Bridge of Alford, a likely site of the ford used by the Covenanters. The flat fields on the near side of the river were the scene of the fighting. Those to the right of the bridge are where the early, decisive engagement between the cavalry of Lord Gordon and Lord Balcarres occurred. Return down the road, following the Royalist charge, and continue straight at the cross-roads. A secondary road to the right, before you reach the bridge, takes you across the eastern side of the battlefield.

The bridge, and the river bank immediately to the north-west of the bridge, provide a view of the Royalists' commanding position on Gallowhill.

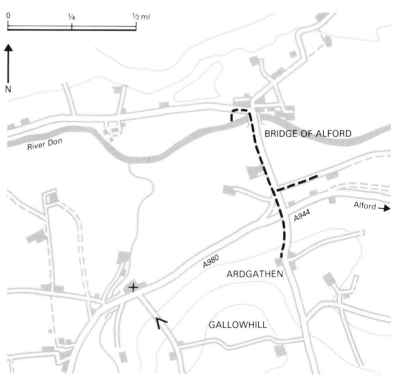

The Battle of Alford

There was no bridge at Alford in 1645. It was obviously extremely dangerous for an army to cross by a ford in full sight of the enemy, but General Baillie decided to take that risk, with disastrous results.

Alford is in the Grampian Region of Scotland, twenty-five miles west of Aberdeen on the A944.

War	The Civil War.
Date	2 July 1645.
Principal commanders	Covenanters: Major-General William Baillie. Royalists: The Earl of Montrose.
Size of armies	Each about 2,000.
Duration	Unknown. Beginning in the morning.
Outcome	Defeat of the Covenanters.
County	Grampian Region (Scotland).
Ord. Survey	1:50,000 map no. 37.
Nat. grid ref.	NJ 5616.

In 1744, labourers cutting peat in the fields south of the River Don near Alford uncovered the well-preserved corpse of a horse and an armour-clad rider. They had been dead for ninety-nine years, and doubtless had enough subterranean companions to form an entire mounted regiment of the dead – all victims of the Battle of Alford.

The miraculous year of the Earl of Montrose was at its height in the early summer of 1645. While in England the Royalist cause received its death-blow at Naseby in Scotland Montrose had the run of the Highlands and was threatening to march south to help the king. In order to assemble a large enough force to accomplish this plan, he sent his right-hand-man, Alasdair MacDonald, to recruit more troops. William Baillie, the Covenanter general who had been avoiding battle with Montrose for several weeks, now saw his opportunity. Without the monstrous MacDonald and a few hundred of his terrifying Irishmen, Baillie reasoned, Montrose would be defanged. Accordingly, he set out south in pursuit of the Royalists, catching up with them near the village of Alford in Aberdeenshire. On the morning of the second of July he drew up within sight of Montrose's army and paused. In front of him was the River Don, a formidable barrier over which he could advance deliberately by way of a ford but which he knew would not lend itself to the haste of even the most orderly retreat. Across the Don were flat, marshy fields, hard going for his large detachment of cavalry. Nearly a mile away beyond Baillie's position rose Gallowhill, where the Royalists waited – such a small body of men that Baillie was tempted to believe they merely formed a rearguard, covering the retreat of the main body of Montrose's army. Urged on by his cavalry commander, Lord Balcarres, Baillie at last decided to ford the Don and drive the Royalists from Gallowhill.

Baillie had been right to hesitate. The entire Royalist army waited on Gallowhill, many of them just out of sight of the Covenanters below. They could not believe their good fortune when they heard that Baillie's army was advancing across the treacherous fields below Gallowhill.

Young Lord Gordon on the Royalist right flank was the first to lose patience and charge. Observing a herd of his father's cattle among the Covenanter's supply train, he swore that he would personally kill General Baillie for his presumption. Gordon led his small body of horsemen down to the levels in such a fierce attack that they nearly turned the entire Covenanter flank with one charge. Lord Balcarres successfully rallied his stunned cavalry, only to find that a band of Irish musketeers had dropped their guns and, with sword and dirks, were among his men, hamstringing and disembowelling their horses. The east side of the battle was nearly over before the centre and west had even engaged.

Lord Aboyne, Lord Gordon's brother, now led a similar cavalry attack from the Royalist left flank. His charge was also followed by a band of Irish infantry, who finished off any

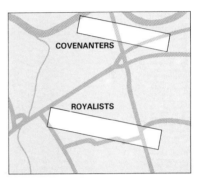

stubborn or disabled Covenanter with what even a Royalist contemporary described as "too little compassion and too much cruelty."

So terror-struck were the Covenanters after these two blows to the right and left of their army that the remainder of the encounter was more a struggle to escape than a battle. Montrose's Highlanders were little kinder than the Irish. With the Covenanters in full flight, they slaughtered at will, in which pursuit they were joined by the servant boys "scarcely fourteen years of age," as a breathless witness recorded. "Young as they were, they thus left an example of a high and noble spirit." Sixteen hundred Covenanters died in this high-spirited blood bath.

The Royalists lost only a handful of men, but among them was young Lord Gordon. The grief of his fellow-soldiers was inordinate. "They seemed more like a beaten army than victors in a battle". "They crowded round his lifeless body, kissing his face and hands". "The Irish wept incessantly for him". And so on. On a field littered with nearly 2,000 corpses the Royalist army wept for one man alone. 131

The Battle of Langport

The Wagg Rhyne is an inconspicuous little stream that flows into the river Yeo just east of Langport in Somerset. In places it is no more than four feet wide, and for much of its length it is concealed by the low shrubs and trees that flourish along its banks. To traffic accelerating out of Langport on the B3153 to Somerton it is no more than a dip in the road and a short stone bridge. To the Parliamentarian soldiers advancing westward in 1645 it was a considerable barrier, the one natural obstacle between them and the last remnants of the western Royalist army. Sir Richard Bulstrode, a Royalist officer looking at the Wagg from the western side, wrote of *"a great marsh and bogg between both armies, which hindered the enemy from attacking us, except by one passage in the bottom of the hill"*. This passage, or ford, across which only four horsemen could ride abreast, appears in retrospect to have been easy to defend. Lord Goring, the Royalist general, sent his musketeers down to the hedgerows at the water's

edge to prevent an attack by the Parliamentarian infantry, and he placed his two cannon on either side of the road, overlooking the ford. He was outnumbered by Sir Thomas Fairfax's army, but was confident of an orderly withdrawal back to Bridgwater.

Goring had not reckoned on the high morale of his opponents, he had failed to notice the flagging spirits of his own men, and his personal conduct was far from inspiring. While admiring his general's ability, Bulstrode deplored his weaknesses, *"for he strangely loved the bottle"* and, even worse, *"his excellency had two companions, who commanded next under him, who fed his wild humours and debauch"*. Having no money to pay his soldiers, Goring gave them license to pillage for a living, thus losing the support of the local populace. Already he had alienated the governor of Langport and could be assured of no sympathy from the town at his back. His army was in a worse position than topographical evidence suggested.

Whether from good tactics, high morale or divine approval, everything

went right for the Parliamentarians that afternoon. By midday they had knocked out the Royalist artillery. Then their musketeers, fighting among the trees and hedges by the water's edge, gained possession of the ford, permitting the cavalry (commanded, but not led, by Cromwell) to charge up the hill toward the waiting Royalists. *"We were at last beaten off, and obliged to a very disorderly retreat,"* wrote the disgruntled Bulstrode. Cromwell received a completely different impression of the engagement. *"To see this is to see the face of God,"* he wrote to Sir Henry Vane.

Wagg Bridge, rebuilt in 1912, spans the likely site of this contested ford. On either side the main road climbs to parallel ridges. Today the land is used for both cattle and crops, and despite the traffic, the whole scene of 1645 is easy to recreate. From the Royalist position, the western slopes, one can leave the main road and still obtain the impression of an unspoiled field. Only the Wagg Rhyne, no more than a trickle now in dry weather, baffles the imagination.

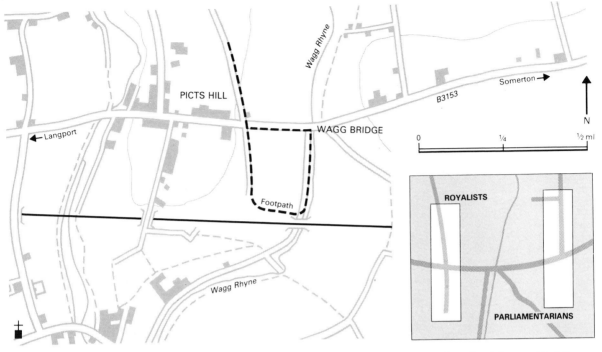

PICTS HILL

Wagg Rhyne

Somerton →

B3153

N

0   ¼   ½ ml

← Langport

WAGG BRIDGE

Footpath

Wagg Rhyne

ROYALISTS

PARLIAMENTARIANS

The B3153 runs through the centre of the field, crossing the Wagg Rhyne between two ridges. In 1645 this was the ford which the Royalists defended.

The battlefield at Langport is on the eastern outskirts of the town. Take the B3153 towards Somerton. In half a mile the road ascends a slight hill then falls away into a little valley. Just as you begin to descend, turn left on a narrow lane. You are now on Pict's Hill, the left flank of the Royalist position. At the bottom of the hill to your right is the Wagg Rhyne and the area where the early stages of the battle were fought by musketeers among the trees and hedges near the stream. Beyond is the opposing ridge, where Sir Thomas Fairfax and Oliver Cromwell drew up on the morning of the tenth of July.

For a brief circuit of the right side of Lord Goring's position, retrace your steps and take the rough farm track immediately opposite leading off the main road. In 300 yards this comes to an end. Turn left down the hill and skirt the railway track until you reach a paved road. Turn left again and return to the main road at Wagg Bridge. To your right, under elders and willows, is the tiny Wagg Rhyne, where the Parliamentarian cavalry were "up to the belly in water". This whole area was marshy and effectively impassable at the time of the battle. At Wagg Bridge, a deep ford 300 years ago, be careful of the traffic, which drives with murderous speed, as if hell-bent on re-enacting the events of 1645.

Langport is in Somerset, four miles west of Somerton, at the junction of the A378 and the A372. The battlefield is half a mile east of the town on the B3153 to Somerton.

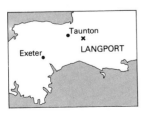

War	The Civil War.
Date	10 July 1645.
Principal commanders	Parliamentarians: Sir Thomas Fairfax. Royalists: Lord Goring.
Size of armies	Parliamentarians: 10,000. Royalists: 7,000.
Duration	Uncertain.
Outcome	Defeat of the Royalists.
County	Somerset.
Ord. Survey	1:50,000 map no. 193.
Nat. grid ref.	ST 4427.

133

The Battle of Sedgemoor

Even in the height of summer there is water on Sedgemoor. Over the centuries sea has changed to swamp and swamp has become damp pasturage, but there is still a sense that just beneath the surface is a body of water waiting its turn to rise again. The drainage ditches, or rhines as they are called in that part of Somerset, confirm this impression. They slice straight across the moor like deep black tracks, though only herons choose to walk along them. In dry seasons they sink beneath a carpet of green, but in winter or in rainy spells the water surges up and threatens to spill out into the fields.

It is a measure of the desperation of James Scott, Duke of Monmouth, that he chose to lead his ragged army against the Royalists over these moors, not only in a wet summer, but at night

in a surprise attack and, according to some historians, in the fog. His gamble ended with death in battle for more than 1,000 of his soldiers and hanging for hundreds of others. Monmouth himself was executed only nine days later. The Battle of Sedgemoor, the last major battle to be fought on English soil, was a miserable, muddy and merciless affair.

Monmouth was the eldest illegitimate son of King Charles II. Because he was a Protestant he became a natural figurehead for Englishmen who feared that the Catholic King James II, Charles II's brother and legitimate heir, would attempt to subvert the Church of England. Exiled in Holland, Monmouth had no burning desire to mount a rebellion, but he was persuaded that the west of England was his for the

taking and that, with help in Scotland from the Earl of Argyll, he would surely become king.

In June 1685 he landed at Lyme Regis, Dorset, and for a few days led an army of enthusiastic but untrained countrymen in bewildering circles through Dorset and Somerset. Then money ran low, and Argyll's rebellion was crushed in the north. Despondent and irresolute, his army dwindling, Monmouth arrived at Bridgwater on the third of July. Two days later a small but well-equipped Government army commanded by Lord Feversham encamped at the village of Westonzoyland, three miles south-east across the moor, and drew up battle lines behind the Bussex Rhine, a crescent-shaped ditch to the north of the town. Realizing that he would have to fight now or

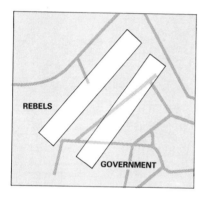

The Battle of Sedgemoor was fought in Somerset, three miles east of Bridgwater and just to the north of the village of Westonzoyland. It is accessible from the A372.

War	Monmouth's Rebellion.
Date	6 July 1685.
Principal commanders	Rebels: The Duke of Monmouth. Government: Lord Feversham.
Size of armies	Rebels: 3,700. Government: 2,500.
Duration	From about 2 until 5 or 6 a.m.
Outcome	Complete suppression of the rebellion. Capture and execution of Monmouth.
County	Somerset.
Ord. Survey	1:50,000 map no. 182.
Nat. grid ref.	ST 3535.

The distant church tower of Westonzoyland rises above the low plain of Sedgemoor (above). No such feature was visible to Monmouth on his ill-fated night march.

Drainage ditches (below) still cut through the fields of Sedgemoor. The Bussex Rhine has disappeared, but the spirit of the place remains unchanged.

surrender, Monmouth resolved upon a night attack and set out shortly before midnight on the evening of the fifth of July. *"His look was sad and full of evil augury,"* said the omniscient historian Macaulay. His army of nearly 4,000 had nothing to smile about either as they headed out across the boggy, black fields. Each soldier was sworn to kill the man next to him if he uttered a word, a severe order that was totally effective until someone, probably one of Feversham's scouts, fired a pistol shot while the rebel army was laboriously crossing the Langmoor Rhine. Fearing that he had lost the element of surprise, Monmouth ordered Lord Grey and his cavalry on ahead to attack the enemy's right flank, while he hastened with his infantry towards the Government line over a mile away. Almost immediately Grey encountered a band of enemy cavalry, riding from Chedzoy back to Westonzoyland. A chaotic skirmish ensued, and in the darkness Grey's force scattered. Only 300 of them reached the bridge over the Bussex Rhine, where they were forced back by the defending cavalry. Monmouth's infantry fared even worse. Upon confronting the enemy, they fired wildly into the night across the rhine until they ran low in ammunition. No more was forthcoming. Alarmed by the first reports of battle, the ammunition column had fled.

Many battles end with nightfall. The Battle of Sedgemoor ended with the light. As soon as they could see their opponents, the disciplined Government soldiers fired with deadly accuracy, then crossed the rhine and brought the battle to a brutal close.

Sedgemoor's face has changed since the seventeenth century. The Langmoor and Bussex Rhines have been replaced by other ditches, so it is impossible to say exactly where the armies stood. But the bleak, damp spirit of the place undoubtedly remains the same. The church towers of Chedzoy and Westonzoyland face each other like sentinels of opposing armies across the plain; a weathered little battle monument hunches behind a fence of concrete and scaffolding; a row of modern cottages stare defensively across to Chedzoy; the water lies black and still by the side of every path.

Monmouth's night-time march can be followed most of the way by public foot-paths. It is a melancholy expedition, but an effective antidote for anyone afflicted with romantic notions of war.

135

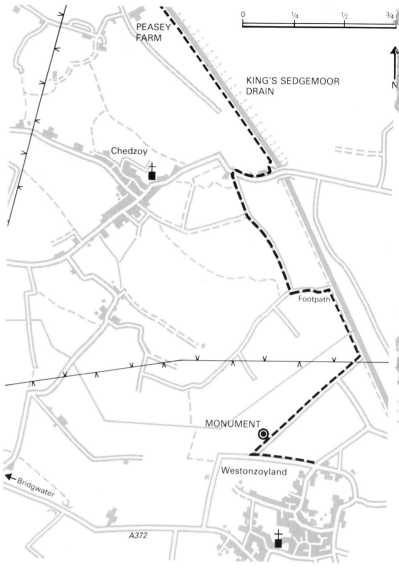

A gloomy clump of stones in the middle of the field commemorates the Battle of Sedgemoor and what seems a curiously random selection of other engagements, including Waterloo and The Great War.

From Bridgwater take the A372 for Yeovil. In slightly over three miles you reach Westonzoyland, where the church should be your first stop. After the battle several hundred rebel prisoners, some of them mortally wounded, were locked up here. It is unlikely that many were in a condition to appreciate the glorious wooden roof. Leaflets about the battle are available in the church.

Continue along the main road for 500 yards and turn left at the end of the town. In just under a mile a dirt track sign-posted to the battlefield leads straight across the flat fields. In wet weather this can be extremely muddy (as can all the surrounding moorland). In a quarter mile you are at the centre of the field, now no longer defined by the arc of Bussex Rhine. It is impossible to say

exactly where Feversham's army awaited

Monmouth. A monotonous arrangement of hedges, ditches and trees serve to confuse the visitor rather than to orient him. Even the battle monument is hidden away behind a clump of trees, 200 yards down a track to the right. It is a sad little memorial, attended by four staddle stones on which the names of other conflicts (curiously including Trafalgar, The Great War and Sedgemoor again) are carved.

A walk of about three and a half miles from Peasy Farm to the battlefield follows roughly the route of Monmouth's silent night-time march, and is well worth taking in the (dry) daylight, though only if there is someone to meet you at the other end. Leave Bridgwater by car on the A39 Glastonbury road. After crossing the M5 motorway take your second right, in about half a mile. Just before this road crosses the

broad, steep-sided King's Sedgemoor Drain, set out on foot to the right along the edge of the drain. In just over a mile turn right on a paved road, then left in a quarter mile down a farm track. From here, midway between Chedzoy and Westonzoyland, the two church towers are both clearly visible. At the end of this track turn left and then right along the drain again. Just before a power line crosses your path, turn sharp right and follow the black straight track to the monument and the battlefield. It is well worth walking at least a portion of this route in either direction, as it gives a remarkable impression of an especially atmospheric battlefield.

The Admiral Blake Museum in Bridgwater has a room devoted to Sedgemoor. The museum is open Tuesday to Saturday 11-4; closed Sunday and Monday.

The beautiful church at Westonzoyland (above) was a temporary prison for hundreds of rebels after the battle.

The village of Chedzoy is two miles north-west of Westonzoyland. On the eve of the battle it was occupied by a party of Royalist soldiers. Its church tower (left), like the tower of Westonzoyland, is a conspicuous landmark.

137

The Massacre at Glen Coe

Even by Highland standards Glen Coe is a spectacular place. Eight miles from east to west, its floor creates a gentle roadway for the River Coe on its way to Loch Leven. But on either side of this peaceful ribbon of meadow and stream abruptly rise the highest mountains of Argyllshire.

It was threatening snow on the night of the twelfth of February 1692 when Captain Robert Campbell of Glen Lyon, stationed in Glen Coe, received a letter from a senior officer. *"You are hereby ordered to fall upon the rebels, the MacDonalds of Glenco, and to put to the sword all under seventy,"* he read. *"You are to have a special care that the old fox and his sons do upon no account escape your hands."* This order was a complete surprise to Campbell. For two weeks the MacDonalds had been generous hosts, sharing their cottages and provisions with his 120 men. They had competed at sports during the day and had played cards and drunk together at night. Campbell may have wondered at the ruthlessness of this command. But if he had second thoughts, common sense soon prevailed. He was sixty years old and in desperate financial straits, having gambled and drunk away his money and lands in his native Glen Lyon. The army, which he had joined only a few months before, was the one brake to his descent into complete disgrace and poverty. Besides, the MacDonalds were traditionally bitter enemies of the Campbells, and he must have heard that *"the old fox"*, Alasdair MacDonald, had proudly withheld his oath of allegiance to William III, the new king, until after the deadline that had been imposed. Campbell had every reason, apart from common humanity, to obey these peremptory orders. As far as he was concerned, two weeks of friendship were insufficient cause for the sacrifice of his livelihood and possibly his life.

At five the next morning, as snow

Glen Coe is on the A82, forty miles north-east of Oban in the Highland Region of Scotland.

Date	13 February 1692.
County	Highland Region.
Ord. Survey	1:50,000 map no. 41.
Nat. grid ref.	NN 1256.

whirled about the glen, he and his officers gave the order to their startled troops: kill without quarter. One party went immediately to the house of old Alasdair, whom they shot as he was struggling into his clothes. They "spared" his wife, tearing the rings off her fingers with their teeth, stripping her naked and throwing her out into the snow. Campbell himself set upon his hosts, tying up nine men, dragging them outside and shooting them on a dunghill. He hesitated to murder a twelve year-old who clutched at his knees, but an assiduous fellow officer shot the lad instead. Some were burned or cut to pieces in their beds; others were hacked down as they ran from their doors.

But for all its bloody intentions, the massacre at Glen Coe was a dreadful failure. Of nearly 400 inhabitants only thirty-eight were murdered. The same number again died in the cruel storm, but the majority, including Alasdair's two sons, escaped. A bungled plan, bad weather and even compassion among the murderers allowed most of the MacDonalds to escape.

A public outcry which followed the massacre failed to bring any of the real villians to justice. The Minister of State for Scotland and King William himself were so deeply involved that any inquiry was doomed to failure.

As for Robert Campbell, he found a familiar refuge behind the brass buttons and scarlet tunic of the army. *"I'd dirk any man if the king gave me orders,"* was his surly self-defence.

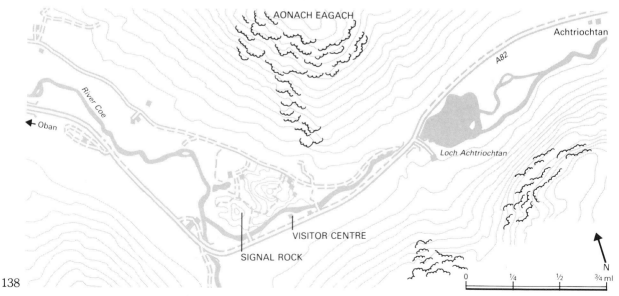

Glen Coe (not to be confused with the modern village of Glencoe) is now a major tourist route. The A82, the main north-south road from Glasgow to Inverness, runs the length of the valley beside the River Coe, giving over 100,000 tourists a year access to the modern visitor centre at the eastern end of the pass. Distances from the centre are Fort William thirty miles, Oban forty miles and Glasgow eighty miles. The centre is an excellent base for any exploration of the Glen and provides the tourist with a wealth of recreational, geological and historical information.

In 1692 Glen Coe contained a number of small settlements; today it is nearly empty. None of the seventeenth-century houses remain, but the MacDonalds are thought to have inhabited a stretch of the valley from Loch Levin in the west to Achtrioctan in the east, a distance of about four miles. One place that is traditionally associated with the massacre is Signal Hill, a wooded knoll just to the west of the visitor centre. On its

Glen Coe (above) was a relatively populous place in 1692; the MacDonalds inhabited a large area of the valley. Today, except for campers in summer, the glen is nearly empty.

The shallow River Coe (right) flows the length of the glen, pausing only at Loch Achtriochtan.

summit at five a.m. on the thirteenth of February, Campbell's soldiers are said to have lit a bonfire to signal the beginning of the massacre. In the snow it is unlikely to have been very effective.

The Aonach Eagach, a solid wall of mountain to the north of the glen, almost certainly prevented the MacDonalds escaping in that direction, but numerous little valleys to the south (most of them cul de sacs) probably provided temporary shelter for the refugees.

Glen Coe is an ideal base for mountain walks and climbs. The visitor centre supplies detailed information.

It is open 17 April to 17 May and 14 September to 11 October, daily 10-5; 18 May to 13 September, 10-7.

139

The Battle of Sheriffmuir

On the morning of the thirteenth of November 1715, the church at Logie in Stirlingshire collected only £1/15, well below their Sunday average. Three miles to the east, the church at Alva did not hold a service at all "*on account of the Batell of Sheriffmuir*".

Ever since the sixth of September, when supporters of Prince James Francis Edward Stuart, claimant to the Scottish throne, had openly declared rebellion, those who lived in the vicinity of Stirling and Dumblane had been in a state of tense anticipation. It was just a matter of time before a Jacobite army under the Earl of Mar would descend from Perth and attempt to break through the Government defences of the Duke of Argyll at Stirling. Mar's strength was rumoured to be enormous and ever-increasing – a fearsome mob of semi-disciplined Highlanders. Argyll had only 3,000 men. The inhabitants of Stirlingshire had no great love for the Government army, but nor had they any particular confidence in the good behaviour of their own countrymen.

When the Duke of Argyll received information that Mar was advancing with 10,000 men, he marched his army to the rough, open ground above Dumblane, land where local militias had long trained and which had thus become known as Sheriffmuir. Argyll hoped to force Mar into battle before the Jacobites could cross the River Forth, and so thwart their intended invasion of England.

The field he chose was moorland dotted with a few poor farms. The land sloped to the south towards a swampy area bordering the Wharry Burn. In the west it fell away to Dumblane and the Allan Water, while to the east rose the wild Ochil Hills. Today Sheriffmuir is even less populous than in 1715. Its western slopes are overgrown with conifers (and new plantations are springing up) but the battlefield is still a splendid stretch of open land. Unfortunately, neither Mar nor Argyll had any chance to take stock of their positions before the battle began. Mar, who outnumbered Argyll three to one, was delighted to accept what he saw as an invitation to annihilate his enemy at one stroke. In approaching Sheriffmuir, however, he was out of sight of the Government forces, and when his men appeared on the field, they discovered that their line stretched slightly to the north of Argyll's. As a consequence, the right flank of each army overlapped the left flank of the other.

Sheriffmuir is in the Central Region of Scotland, six miles north of Stirling.

War	The First Jacobite Rebellion.
Date	13 November 1715.
Principal commanders	Government: The Duke of Argyll. Jacobites: The Earl of Mar.
Size of armies	Government: 3,000. Jacobites: 10,000.
Duration	From midday until dusk.
Outcome	Inconclusive, though a moral victory for the smaller Government force.
County	Central Region (Scotland).
Ord. Survey	1:50,000 map no. 57.
Nat. grid ref.	NN 8201.

Both generals exploited this lop-sided position with impetuous, simultaneous charges against the outflanked left flank of the opposing army. Mar's men had not even fully assembled on their left before the Government dragoons, galloping with ease over the surprisingly frozen marsh, were upon them. The Highlanders put up a brave resistance, but the well-equipped dragoons on their formidable horses (far stronger than the Highland breed) forced them back two miles over the next three hours. Argyll accompanied this victorious wing of his army and, not having seen anything of the rest of the battle, returned to Sheriffmuir imagining that he had won the day.

This was far from the case. After firing a devastating volley into the Government ranks, the Highlanders on the right flank of Mar's army had dropped their guns and overwhelmed their opponents in less than ten minutes. The bloody pursuit continued

down into Dumblane and almost as far as Stirling, over five miles away. They too arrived back at the battlefield confident of victory.

Until dark that day the remains of both armies glared at each other over the corpse-cluttered moor. It was the Earl of Mar who made the first move. Although he acknowledged only sixty casualties he withdrew first from the field, leaving Argyll's shattered army in possession of Sheriffmuir.

Both generals claimed victory, but the truth more likely lies in the song that appeared soon after the battle:

There's some say that we wan,
And some say that they wan,
And some say that nane wan at a'
man.·

James Stuart, known as 'The Old Pretender', was left in little doubt as to who had won. When he arrived from France a month later, his army was in tatters, his generals disillusioned and his rebellion lost.

Sheriffmuir is still mostly open land but there are indications that infant plantations of conifers may soon grow up to obscure at least the northern part of the battlefield. Until then it provides a view that would be recognizable to any Highlander or red-coat who strayed back from the dead.

From Stirling take the A9 towards Dumblane and turn right on a secondary road to Blackford in about two miles, just past Stirling University. This narrow road winds up to the moorland that climbs towards the Ochil Hills. In about three and a half miles turn left on another small road leading to Dumblane. You are now facing west as did the Jacobites in 1715. Their army very likely lined up across this path in battle formation at a point a quarter of a mile or so past the turning. There are few geographical features to go on in reconstructing this battle. The little Wharry Burn, down the slope to your left, protected (or would have protected if it had not been frozen over) the left flank of the Jacobite line. Ahead of you to the north of the road,

is the dark mass of a conifer plantation, the corner of which marks the approximate location of the Government left flank.

Continue along the road to the plantation. The area on your left, down by the burn, is the scene of the Government success. To the right, across the brow of the moor, is where the Jacobites routed the left of the Government line.

The only battle monument is a large cairn on the right of the road where the woods take over from moorland. This was erected in memory of the clan Macrae, who suffered heavily on the left of the Jacobite line. From the cairn a path leads along the stone wall which forms a border between woodland and moorland. In 200 yards there is an excellent view diagonally across the field from north-west to south-east, though the magnificent hills beyond may prove too distracting a background for any purely military observations.

In the woods north of the cairn is the Gathering Stone, but a snow storm prevented this author from finding it.

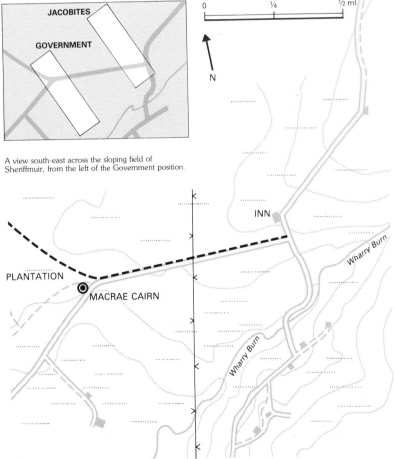

A view south-east across the sloping field of Sheriffmuir, from the left of the Government position.

JACOBITES

GOVERNMENT

N

0   ¼   ½ ml

INN

PLANTATION

MACRAE CAIRN

Wharry Burn

Wharry Burn

The Battle of Glen Shiel

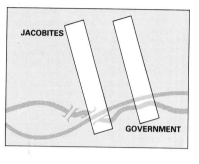

The rebellion fought by supporters of James Stuart in 1719 consisted of one battle and fewer than 100 casualties. Yet it cost a small fortune, involved half a dozen European countries and took many months of preparation and intrigue. The sorry climax to this undertaking was the Battle of Glen Shiel.

It began as an idea of Cardinal Alberoni, the man who effectively ruled Spain from 1715-20. At war with England in 1718, he chose to adopt a subversive means of warfare (one still popular today) by supporting some disaffected faction within the enemy country. His cause was not hard to find. Only three years earlier Prince James Stuart, claimant to the British throne, had lost his brief rebellion. As Alberoni knew, however, there was still considerable Jacobite sympathy in south-west England and in Scotland. With the exiled Duke of Ormonde he planned a major "Stuart" invasion of Britain, sponsored and supplied by the Spanish government. In March 1719 a fleet of twenty-nine ships left Cadiz. Five thousand soldiers formed the core of the expedition, but there were arms enough for the 30,000 rebels who were confidently expected to join the cause in England. Within a few days of setting out, a storm of Old Testament malice completely crippled the fleet, driving it back to Spain. As far as Cardinal Alberoni was concerned, his Stuart adventure was finished.

But the adventure was only just beginning for a tiny expedition of Scots and Spaniards, whose plan had been to create a diversion in Scotland while the larger fleet invaded England. They landed first at the Isle of Lewis, then advanced cautiously to the mainland, where they dithered at Loch Alsh over whether to advance to Inverness or to wait for word about the fortunes of the southern expedition. The English navy finally made up their minds for them, forcing them inland through the

narrow pass at Glen Shiel, where a Government army under General Wightman was advancing from the south-east. By now the Jacobites had increased their numbers with Highland recruits, but with far fewer than they had expected. *"Not above a thousand men appeared, and even those seemed not very fond of the enterprise,"* wrote James Keith, younger brother of the Earl Marischal, the expedition's leader.

The River Shiel finds its way to the sea between some of the highest mountains in Scotland, and where the Jacobites chose to meet the Government army was the narrowest, most defensible place in this precipitous ravine. The odds were entirely in their favour. Not only did they outnumber their enemy, but they were Scotsmen familiar with hill fighting, facing an army that included English and Dutch. Yet such was the ebb of their spirit that the rebels scarcely put up a fight at all.

Wightman's men opened fire on the Jacobite right flank shortly after five p.m. on the tenth of June. The Jacobites responded by withdrawing to a stronger position farther down the Glen. Then the Government soldiers turned to the left and centre of the rebel line. Here the Jacobites held the north slopes of the glen up to a dizzying height, yet here also they were driven back by the resolute advance of the Government. Seaforths, MacKintoshes, Campbells and MacKenzies scrambled for safety over the mountains. Only the centre of the line, stiffened by 200 puzzled Spaniards, managed to hold its ground.

The next day these Spaniards, deserted by their allies, surrendered to General Wightman. *"Everybody else,"* said the bitter James Keith, *"took the road he liked best."*

Confronted by such a wild landscape, it is a wonder that the Government soldiers did not turn and run. They not only stayed, but won the battle with ease.

Glen Shiel is in the Highland Region of Scotland. The A87 runs along its length.

War	The Jacobite Rebellion of 1719.
Date	10 June 1719.
Principal commanders	Government: Major-General Wightman. Jacobites: The Earl Marischal.
Size of armies	Government: 1,100. Jacobites: About 1,500.
Duration	From late afternoon until dusk.
Outcome	Defeat of the Jacobites and the end of their rebellion.
County	Highland Region (Scotland).
Ord. Survey	1:50,000 map no. 33.
Nat. grid ref.	NG 9913.

A cairn to the north of the road marks the traditional site for the Battle of Glen Shiel.

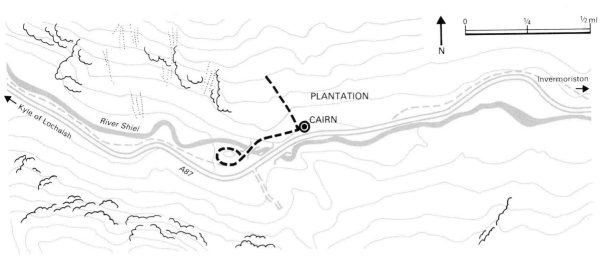

A Walk around the pass at Glen Shiel demands tough shoes, good lungs and a head for heights. Those lacking any of the above can still marvel at this most spectacular and precipitous of battlefields from the side of the A87.

From Invermoriston, on Loch Ness, drive west along the A887 and continue towards Kyle of Lochalsh on the A87. Six miles west of the Cluanie Inn at the head of Loch Cluanie, the conifer plantations on the slopes at the right of the road abruptly end.

The armies faced each other on the steep northern slopes of Glen Shiel (left). Lowlanders fighting for the Government had no difficulty with the rough terrain.

A short cairn and a blue sign here on the right mark the generally accepted site of the battle. The exact site is arguable.

Both Jacobite and Government forces were deployed mainly to the north of the road, the side of the cairn. (There seems no clear reason for this.) The Jacobites, facing east, likely chose to defend the narrowest point, where a ridge in the northern slope constricts the pass to little more than fifty yards. Their army of approximately 1,500 men stretched about half a mile up the hill. It is extraordinarily difficult to imagine thousands of soldiers clambering along these steep and desolate slopes, but

here, as in few other battlefields, there is an opportunity for the visitor to experience identical conditions to those faced by the armies in 1719. There is only one way to inspect the field – go straight up the north slope. The few aimless tracks are made by sheep, who are generally unconcerned with military history, but the rocks and heather make sure, if rough, footing. On these slopes the feat of advancing to battle diminishes when one considers the awesome difficulties involved in retreating.

The mountains to the west absorbed the retreating Jacobites. Only two hundred Spaniards, bewildered by their surroundings, were forced to surrender.

The Battle of Falkirk

At the end of December 1746 a new English general arrived in Edinburgh with every confidence of crushing the Jacobite rebellion of Prince Charles Edward Stuart. General Henry Hawley had no respect for the Highlanders who formed the bulk of the Prince's army. *"I do and always shall despise these rascals,"* he said, and he gave his troops a simple lesson in how to meet a Highland charge: *"The sure way to demolish them is at three deep to fire by ranks diagonally to the centre".* Eager to put his theories into practice, Hawley marched west to Falkirk and by the sixteenth of January was poised to attack the Jacobites, who were besieging Stirling Castle. Here he showed uncharacteristic hesitation. Was he unsure of his next move or overconfident of an easy victory? Or was he really seduced, as some historians attest, by the Countess of Kilmarnock,

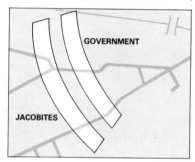

"a woman of splendid person and manners", whose husband was a well-known Jacobite and whose hospitality to this enemy general was curiously lavish? At any rate, when anxious Government scouts reported that the Highlanders were massing to the south of the town, General Hawley was still with his hostess at Callendar House. He arrived at the gallop, surprised and dishevelled at about two o'clock in the afternoon and ordered his army to march up the steep hill to Falkirk Moor, where the Jacobites had already seized the highest land.

Hawley and his officers had never set foot on the field where the Jacobites awaited them, although it was only a mile from their camp. Falkirk Moor is now pastureland, enclosed by hedges and fences, its views partly obscured by woods and avenues of beeches. In 1746 it was open land, clearly visible to those citizens of Falkirk who crowded up the steeple of their town hall to watch the battle. They saw the Highlanders forming a line from north to south, their left wing protected from the

advancing English by a steep ravine which scarred the north face of the descent to Falkirk. The centre of the Highland army occupied a hill about 400 feet high. From there, out of sight of the spectators, the line stretched down a gradual slope to where boggy land bordering the little Glen Burn protected them from an outflanking manoeuvre. This was how the English army discovered the Highlanders when they finally struggled up the hill to Falkirk Moor. To add to their misfortunes, they had been forced to abandon their heavy guns in the mud along the track. And now it began to rain, a fierce south-westerly gale driving into their faces.

The two armies stood no more than 300 yards apart. To the Government soldiers' surprise, the Highlanders did not launch one of their reckless attacks. Painstakingly disciplined by Lord George Murray, they waited patiently for the English to make a move. This was not long in coming. General Hawley, as contemptuous as ever of his opponents, commanded the dragoons of his left flank to attack the Highlanders. With extraordinary self-control the Scotsmen waited until the riders were within fifteen yards, then opened up a withering fire that instantly turned the orderly advance into a savage rout. Dropping their firearms, the Highlanders charged the dragoons with dirks and claymores, disembowelling horses and then hacking the terrified riders to death. Those dragoons that could save themselves galloped back to Falkirk, followed by the Scots, who had forgotten Lord George Murray's stern orders to stay put. Half the battle was over before the Government army had even completely assembled.

Emboldened by their success on the right, the Stewarts and Camerons on the left flank now let out a fierce battle cry and charged across the ravine. The Government forces retreated down the hill towards Falkirk but rallied and counter-attacked so successfully that they drove the Highland left flank from the field. Unfortunately for the Government army, their commander had had enough warfare and weather for one afternoon. Within half an hour of the first shot Hawley had retreated from Falkirk Moor along with most of his army. He was later to claim that he had given *"a severe check to the Highlanders"*, but he did not dine with Lady Kilmarnock at Callendar House that evening.

Falkirk is in the Central Region of Scotland, ten miles south of Stirling. It is at the junction of the A904 and the A803.

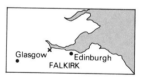

War	The Second Jacobite Rebellion.
Date	17 January 1746.
Principal commanders	Government: General Henry Hawley. Jacobites: Prince Charles Edward Stuart Lord George Murray.
Size of armies	The Jacobites about 8,000, slightly outnumbered by the Government.
Duration	Less than half an hour, starting at about 4 p.m.
Outcome	Defeat of the Government army.
County	Central Region (Scotland).
Ord. Survey	1:50,000 map no. 65.
Nat. grid ref.	NS 8678.

The Battle of Falkirk was fought on wild moorland to the south of the city. Today the area consists of enclosed pastureland interspersed with stands of mature trees. This avenue of beeches (left) grows on high land once occupied by Prince Charles's army.

A canal and a railway now interpose themselves between the city of Falkirk and the high ground to the south-west, where the battle of 1746 was fought. The arduous route of the bedraggled Government army from the town to the battlefield is now impossible to trace, but the field itself is relatively unspoiled.

From Falkirk take the B803 towards Slamannan. 600 yards after crossing the railway tracks bear right on Lochgreen Road. In half a mile turn right again. The battle monument is straight ahead. This marks the head of the ravine, which plunges down towards the canal. In 1746 it separated the left flank of the Jacobite army from the right of the Government forces. The Highlanders were driven from this position by a fierce Government counter-attack. A path leads down the east (the Government) side of this ravine from the monument. At the bottom there is a pleasant track along the canal. The ravine is now totally overgrown. A little brook flows down it, seemingly unequal to the task of carving out such a gully.

Walk back to Lochgreen Road, turn right and then immediately left down an avenue of beeches. The high ground to your left is that occupied by the centre of the Jacobite army, who arrived on the moor first and had the pick of the land. Continue along this path until you reach the B803. Ahead the land slopes down to Glen Burn, which protected the right of the Highland army. Turn left and walk along the road for 200 yards. Then turn left again through a gate and walk up across the fields. These are now pastureland but were open moorland at the time of the battle. This path takes you over the right centre of the Jacobite position and down into the depression that separated the two armies. There is still marshy ground here, but the little brook (the same one which flows down the ravine) has been dug out to form an effective drainage ditch. In 1746, on a rainy day in midwinter, this low area was a murderous swamp, especially for cavalry. The higher ground ahead and to your right is likely that held by General Hawley's Government troops.

This path leads back to Lochgreen Road, 200 yards away from the turning to the monument.

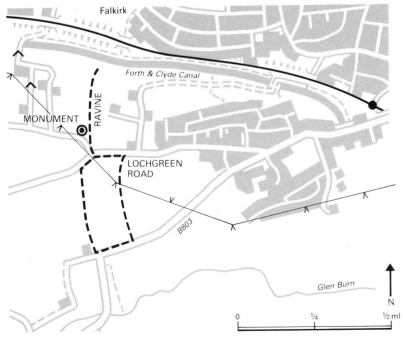

147

The old Leneach Farmhouse, around which the fighting raged in 1746, is now a battle museum at the information centre. Along with the cairns, the graves and the car park, it occupies the small part of the field that is not a forest.

The Battle of Culloden

Any serious hopes of reestablishing the Stuarts on the British throne died in 1746 on a rainswept moor five miles east of Inverness. Any romantic notions of gallantry, nationalism or rules of war should also have been among the casualties at the Battle of Culloden, one of the most brutal events in British history.

In mid-February 1746 Prince Charles Edward Stuart, grandson of King James II and claimant to the thrones of England and Scotland, withdrew to Inverness. Despite an abortive invasion of England, in the late autumn, Bonnie Prince Charlie's seven-month-old rebellion had surprisingly prospered. His spirited army of Highlanders had defeated King George II's forces at Prestonpans and

Falkirk. Now, in the depth of winter, the confident Jacobites continued to harry the English, while waiting for the change of weather that would permit a full-scale campaign.

One hundred miles to the southeast, in Aberdeen, an awesome Government force was gathering. Its commander was William Duke of Cumberland, the second son of George II. He was only twenty-four, four months younger than Charles (though at eighteen stone, he substantially outweighed his opponent). Cumberland was determined to avenge the humiliations of his three predecessors and in this aim he had the full backing of an English government increasingly worried about the Jacobite successes.

Cumberland moved quickly. With the first hint of spring his army of 9,000 marched towards Inverness, crossing the River Spey unopposed and reaching the town of Nairn on the fourteenth of April. The Jacobites were astonished to discover that a battle was so imminent. They hastily recalled what men they could and gathered on Drummossie Moor (now called Culloden Moor) a flat stretch of grazing land near Culloden House. *"There could never be more improper ground for Highlanders,"* said Lord George Murray, the Prince's ablest general. But Charles was a poor tactician and chose to listen to men who were no better generals than himself.

The Jacobites' confusion on the brink of battle was augmented by a

148

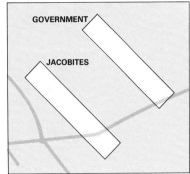

The battlefield of Culloden is in the Highland Region of Scotland, five and a half miles east of Inverness on the B9006.

War	The Second Jacobite Rebellion.
Date	16 April 1746.
Principal commanders	Government: The Duke of Cumberland. Jacobites; Prince Charles Edward Stuart.
Size of armies	Government: 9,000. Jacobites: 5,000.
Duration	Less than an hour in early afternoon.
Outcome	Complete defeat of the Jacobites and an end to their rebellion.
County	Highland Region (Scotland).
Ord. Survey	1:50,000 map no. 27.
Nat. grid ref.	NH 7445.

daring but disastrous plan to surprise the English in a night attack on the fifteenth of April. They marched through the darkness in increasing disarray then, within two miles of Nairn, heard a distant drum-beat that indicated the English were on guard. Exhausted by this march of nearly twenty miles, the Scots arrived back at Culloden at dawn. They scarcely had time to snatch an hour of sleep or a bite of food when word came that the Government forces were advancing rapidly upon them.

The Battle of Culloden lasted less than an hour. Five thousand Jacobites lined up by clans on the south-west of the field, the men tired and famished, the generals dispirited, the gunners inexperienced and the cavalry practically non-existent. Five hundred yards across the moor was the formidable army of Cumberland – well-trained,

well-fed and eager for battle. Even the weather favoured the English. The rain, which now began to fall, was driven into the faces of the Scots by a cruel north-easterly wind.

Shortly after one o'clock Prince Charles ordered his cannon to open fire. This was answered by a devastating and continuous blast from the Government ordnance, which tore great gaps through the Scottish line for nearly twenty minutes. As a result of this suicidal hesitancy, when the order finally came for the Jacobites to attack, the battle was all but lost. The right wing of the Highland army managed to reach the Government line, where they were overwhelmed by superior numbers. The left wing, who had slightly farther to charge, never succeeded in engaging the enemy at all, but crumpled before disciplined and unceasing volleys of musket fire.

Cumberland's horsemen then moved out around both flanks to cut down the retreating Scotsmen. The rout of the Jacobites was complete.

The carnage, however, had scarcely begun. Cumberland, as if piqued by such an easy victory, encouraged the grossest savagery towards all Scots, whether soldier or civilian. The wounded on the field were murdered and robbed where they lay, prisoners were shot and leaders were publicly executed. *"This generation must be pretty well wore out before this country will be quiet,"* wrote Cumberland, who returned to London that summer as a national hero – "Billy the Martial Boy", "Sweet William", Baron Culloden.

The Scots, who now suffered the long and brutal policy of "pacification", saw him in a different light, and have known him to this day as "Butcher" Cumberland. 149

Most of the field at Culloden is covered with a dense pine plantation (above). This deprives the visitor of a splendid view, for the moor, although flat, is on high land overlooking the Moray Firth. Clearing of the forest is scheduled to begin in 1982.

Beyond the wall which marks the forest's boundary to the south of the field (below), the land more nearly resembles the treeless moor of 1746. It was on this side of the Jacobite line, their right flank, that the Argyll Militia fought and fell.

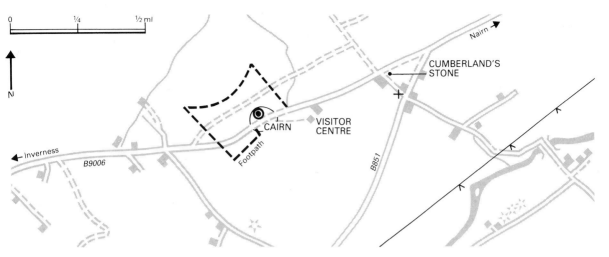

To reach Culloden, leave Inverness on the A96 towards Nairn, turn right on the A9 and then left on the B9006. The visitor centre and car park are on the right of the road, a distance from Inverness of five miles. Cumberland's Stone, from which the duke surveyed the field, is beside the B9006 a quarter mile west of the centre.

For many years the battlefield of Culloden has been one of the most frustrating historical sites to visit. At some point in the nineteenth century, the bleak and treeless moorland was planted over with the trimmed, untroubled ranks of a conifer plantation. The modern Culloden Centre, which stands in a small patch of open

The Cumberland Stone (below) was the substantial viewpoint for the bulky young Duke of Cumberland. Smaller stones indicate the mass graves of the clans.

ground on the east of the field, supplies the tourist with anything he might need in the way of information but cannot disguise the fact that there is little actually to "see" except memorial stones. The massive cairn, erected in 1881, dominates the roadside to the west of the centre, while beside it, scarcely noticeable at first, are the quiet stones that mark the graves of the clans. This open area, now occupied by the centre and the memorials, was a scene of fierce fighting – the left wing of Cumberland's army and the only part of his line to come into direct contact with the Jacobites.

To "see" the rest of the field you must plunge into the woods on a path to the south of the road beyond the cairn. This leads to the Jacobite line, where the approximate positions of each clan is marked

by a stone. It then cuts across the north of the field and, still in the forest, leads south along the Government line to a point near the car park. Nothing here is as it was except the heather on the marshy forest floor. But the trees maintain a stillness that seems, in such a place, mournfully appropriate.

All this will be changed when the clearing of the forest, scheduled to begin in 1982, restores Culloden Moor to its original state.

The Culloden Centre includes the tiny Leneach Farmhouse, which was standing in 1746 and is now a battlefield museum. The modern information centre contains a book/gift shop and a hall for audio-visual programmes. These two buildings are open daily from 17 April to 28 May and 1 September to 11 October, 9:30-6; 29 May to 31 August, 9:30-8.

The Cumberland Stone.

The Argyll Militia.

Mixed Clans.

Clan Donald.

151

Ruthven Barracks

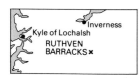

War	The Second Jacobite Rebellion.
County	Highland Region (of Scotland).
Ord. Survey	1:50,00 map no. 35.
Nat. grid ref.	NN 7699.

Ruthven Barracks rise dramatically from the plain south of Kingussie. After Culloden, the Highlanders assembled here, hoping for yet another rallying cry.

Less than a mile to the south of Kingussie stand the ruins of Ruthven Barracks. They occupy a natural position for a fortification – a low hill rising so steeply from the marshy fields by the River Spey that people in the town will tell you it is manmade. For centuries there was a castle here, seat of the Lords of Badenoch, where Alastair Stuart, the ill-famed "Wolf of Badenoch" played chess with the Devil on the night of his death in 1394.

The English army had no such romantic associations with the site. In 1718, determined to enforce their law and order in Scotland after the First Jacobite Rebellion, they built the barracks for a permanent military garrison. Twenty-seven years later Scotland was again in arms and all but thirteen of the soldiers manning the barracks were called north to join General Cope in his attempt to subdue the Jacobite rebels. Within a few days of their departure, a force of 200 Highlanders, eager for action and ravenous from a long march on which they had eaten ,nothing but beef, attacked the tiny garrison. The English defenders, had they known, might have placated the Scots with a few sacks of oatmeal dropped over the walls, but they were too busy at their undermanned defences to contemplate such novel tactics. The Highlanders finally attempted to burn down the gate of the barracks, only to be driven back downhill by the firepower of thirteen men. After three Scots had died in this humbling assault, the rest tightened their belts and limped off. Five months later, in February 1746, a determined force of 300 Jacobites,

confident from their victory at Falkirk, battered the barracks for three days. At last the defenders capitulated and were allowed to march away, though a retreat through the Highlands may well have been worse than imprisonment.

Ruthven Barracks, which saw some of the earliest action in Charles Stuart's brief rebellion, also saw its mournful conclusion. After their defeat at the Battle of Culloden, Lord George Murray and 1,500 Jacobites withdrew to the barracks to await orders from Prince Charles. Their numbers quickly swelled and so, strangely, did their spirits. Though they had little equipment and almost no food, the 4-5,000 Highlanders at Ruthven Barracks were again prepared to face "Butcher" Cumberland in battle. Their leader was not so resilient. *"Let every man seek his safety the best way he can,"* came the despairing final command from Bonnie Prince Charlie.

This message broke the heart of the Jacobite cause. *"The Highlanders gave vent to their grief in wild howlings and lamentations,"* wrote the Chevalier Johnstone. *"The tears flowed down their cheeks when they thought that their country was now at the discretion of the Duke of Cumberland, and on the point of being plundered; whilst they and their children would be reduced to slavery. and plunged, without resource into a state of remediless poverty."*

They blew up Ruthven Barracks before scattering to the uncertain security of the Highlands. It stands today as they left it, a shell of stone high above the marshes of the River Spey.

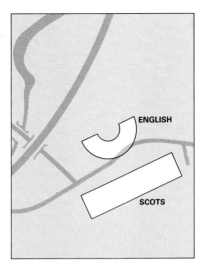

Queen Victoria was not amused by Kingussie. *"A very straggly place with very few cottages,"* she wrote of it when she passed through in 1861. It is now a prosperous town which attracts sightseers in summer and skiers in winter. One of the sights still worth seeing are the ruins of Ruthven Barracks, which stand within a mile of the High Street. From Kingussie take the road to the railway station (on your right if you are driving towards Inverness). Cross the tracks, continue under the new bridge of the A9, and turn left at a T-junction. The barracks are to your left, isolated on their abrupt hill in the middle of a plain.

The ruins consist of two walled structures. The principal enclosure is square and includes two main buildings, each three stories high. These provided living quarters for the 2-300 soldiers who could be garrisoned there. The remains of an oven are still visible in the west corner. A courtyard seventy-five feet by forty feet occupies the space between these principal buildings. The smaller structure to the north included the stables.

It is tempting to imagine the plain around the barracks surrounded by lamenting Highlanders after the Battle of Culloden, but if they had had any sense they would have kept to the higher, drier ground to the south, where the tiny village of Ruthven once stood.

A second, smaller building on the hilltop was probably used for stables. Like the adjacent barracks, it is now a ruin, visited by sheep and the occasional tourist.

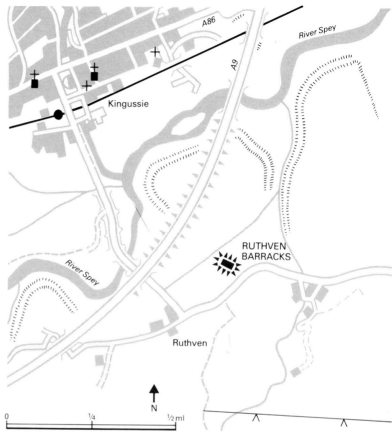

The unkind attentions of over 250 winters have made the stones of Ruthven Barracks seem more the fabric of an ancient Scottish castle than of an English fort.

INDEX

BATTLEFIELD NOTES

Over the past hundred years many authors have attempted to relate topography and military history. Some have been genuine scholars and have made valuable contributions to the field, but most are enthusiasts and popularists, among which this writer must count himself. The danger of such an approach is that the author is easy prey to myths and traditions, some of which became associated with battles long after they were fought. It is tempting for a popularist, when faced with fragmentary or even contradictory contemporary accounts of a battle, to settle for the security of a good story, even if he fears that it may not be true. The notes below indicate the sort of problems that arise in any attempt to present history as entertainment.

Geographical problems involving pre-conquest battlefields result both from a scarcity of contemporary information and from place names that have long since changed. Ashdown and Ethandun can only be established within a few miles. Maldon is one of the most reliable early fields, as its unusual features are ideally suited by Northey Island and the causeway. The site of the Battle of Ashingdon, however, is far from agreed. I have adopted a solution persuasively proposed by A.H. Burne in *More Battlefields of England*.

p36 The Battle of Brander is locally associated with a field to the south of the River Awe, but to make any sense of this engagement it is necessary to situate the opening stages across the river, where the road and railway now lie.

p38 Halidon Hill is an undisputed landmark, but some historians have suggested that the Scottish attack came more from the west, along the route of the present A6105.

p44 Pilleth can be refought in a number of ways. Fifteenth-century Welshmen were apparently more interested in winning their battles than in describing them.

p50 This site for the Battle of Shrewsbury depends entirely upon accepting that the church was built on the battlefield. A minority of historians have rejected this pre-condition and found alternative locations.

p64 It is not at all clear which "three hills" were involved in the Battle of Edgcote. Edgcote Hill is generally accepted as the Yorkist position, but exactly where the Lancastrians encamped prior to the battle is uncertain.

p70 Bosworth Field is an undisputed site for King Richard's last battle, and he is generally believed to have occupied Ambion Hill, but the position of the Lancastrians and especially of the indecisive Stanleys is still a matter of debate.

p74 The exact position of the rebel army at the Battle of Stoke is uncertain, but the hill above East Stoke has been traditionally associated with their defence.

p82 The hill behind which the Scots were concealed at the Battle of Ancrum Moor is locally thought to be Gersit Law, but Peniel Heugh, more than two miles to the east, has its adherents.

p92 There is some confusion about the directions from which the four Royalist parties attacked Stamford Hill, though it seems certain that the south and west slopes figured in the assault.

p106 Reconstructions of the Battle of Cheriton generally ignore that the land has three ridges. This account of the battle is based on the examination of the site by William Seymour who, in *Battles in Britain 1642-1746*, suggested that the Royalists occupied the central ridge and not, as is often thought, the northernmost one.

p122 This version of the Battle of Auldearn is based on Dr. David Stevenson's recent study of the evidence in *Alasdair MacColla and the Highland Problem in the Seventeenth Century*.

p132 The ford on the Wagg Rhyne. is sometimes placed south of the present B3153 bridge. This effectively moves the whole field to a position south of the one described in the text.

FURTHER READING

Many of the works consulted in the preparation of this book are to be found only in a few of the largest reference libraries. The following list suggests a selection of general titles, a number of which are likely to be in local libraries.

Ashley, Maurice, *The English Civil War: A Concise History,* Thames and Hudson, 1974.

Barnett, Correlli, *Britain and Her Army, 1509-1970,* Alan Lane, Penguin Press, 1970.

Barron, Evan, *The Scottish War of Independence,* J. Nisbit, 1914.

Barrow, G.W.S., *Robert Bruce,* Eyre and Spottiswoode, 1965.

Brander, Michael, *Scottish and Border Battles and Ballads,* Seeley, 1975.

Buchan, John, *The Marquis of Montrose,* Nelson, 1913.

Burne, A.H., *Battlefields of England,* Methuen, 1950.

Burne, A.H., *More Battlefields of England,* Methuen, 1952.

Cheetham, Anthony, *The Life and Times of Richard III,* Weidenfeld and Nicolson, 1972.

Donaldson, Gordon, *Scotland: James V to James VII,* Oliver and Boyd, 1974.

Douglas, D.C., *William the Conqueror,* Eyre and Spottiswoode, 1965.

Fergusson, James, *The White Hind,* Faber, 1963.

Fraser, Antonia, *Cromwell – Our Chief of Men,* Weidenfeld and Nicolson, 1973.

Green, Howard, *Guide to the Battlefields of Britain and Ireland,* Constable, 1973.

Kendall, P.M., *Warwick the Kingmaker,* Allen Unwin, 1959.

Labarge, Margaret, *Simon de Montfort,* Eyre and Spottiswoode, 1962.

Mackenzie, Agnes Mure, *The Kingdom of Scotland,* Chambers 1940.

Nicholson, Ranald, *Scotland: The Later Middle Ages,* Oliver and Boyd, 1974.

Oman, Charles, *The Political History of England, 1377-1485,* Longmans, 1910.

Petrie, Charles, *The Jacobite Movement,* Eyre and Spottiswoode, 1959.

Prebble, John, *Glencoe: The Story of the Massacre,* Secker and Warburg, 1966.

Rogers, H.C.B., *Battles and Generals of the Civil Wars, 1642-1651,* Seeley Service, 1968.

Ross, C., *The Wars of the Roses,* Thames and Hudson, 1976.

Scofield, Cora L., *The Life and Reign of Edward IV,* Longmans, 1923.

Seymour, William, *Battles in Britain,* Vols. 1-2, Sidgwick and Jackson, 1975.

Simons, Eric N., *The Reign of Edward IV,* Muller, 1966.

Stenton, F.M., *Anglo-Saxon England,* Clarendon Press, 1943.

Tayler, Alistair and Henrietta, *1715: Story of the Rising,* Nelson, 1936.

Tomasson, Katherine and Francis Buist, *Battles of the '45,* Batsford, 1962.

Trench, Charles Chevenix, *The Western Rising,* Methuen, 1950.

Woolrych, Austin, *Battles of the English Civil War,* Batsford, 1961.

Young, Peter and John Adair, *Hastings to Culloden,* G. Bell, 1964.